Become a top fact-fetcher with CGP!

Quick question — do you own CGP's
Knowledge Organiser for AQA GCSE Chemistry?

You do? Great! Now you can use this Knowledge Retriever
to check you've really remembered all the crucial facts.

There are two memory tests for each topic, plus mixed quiz questions
to make extra sure it's all stuck in your brain. Enjoy.

CGP — still the best! ☺

Our sole aim here at CGP is to produce the highest quality books —
carefully written, immaculately presented and dangerously close to being funny.

Then we work our socks off to get them out to you
— at the cheapest possible prices.

Contents

How to Use This Book..................................2

Working Scientifically
The Scientific Method..................................3
Designing & Performing Experiments........5
Presenting Data...7
Conclusions, Evaluations and Units............9
Mixed Practice Quizzes.............................11

Topic 1 — Atomic Structure and the Periodic Table
Atoms, Elements and Compounds.............13
Equations, Mixtures & Chromatography...15
More Separation Techniques....................17
Atomic and Electronic Structure...............19
Mixed Practice Quizzes............................21
The Periodic Table....................................23
Metals and Non-Metals............................25
Group 1 and Group 0 Elements..............27
Group 7 Elements....................................29
Mixed Practice Quizzes............................31

Topic 2 — Bonding, Structure and Properties of Matter
Ions and Ionic Bonding............................33
Covalent Bonding & Simple Molecules..35
Covalent Structures..................................37
Mixed Practice Quizzes............................39
Metallic Bonding......................................41
States of Matter and Changing State......43
Nanoparticles and their Uses...................45
Mixed Practice Quizzes............................47

Topic 3 — Quantitative Chemistry
Mass and the Mole...................................49
Moles, Equations & Limiting Reactants..51
Gases and Concentrations.......................53
Atom Economy and Percentage Yield.......55
Mixed Practice Quizzes............................57

Topic 4 — Chemical Changes
Acids, Bases and their Reactions..............59
Strong and Weak Acids............................61
Reactivity of Metals..................................63
Redox Reactions and Ionic Equations.......65
Electrolysis...67
Mixed Practice Quizzes............................69

Topic 5 — Energy Changes
Endothermic & Exothermic Reactions........71
Cells, Batteries and Fuel Cells..................73
Mixed Practice Quizzes............................75

Topic 6 — The Rate and Extent of Chemical Change
Rates of Reaction.....................................77
Factors Affecting Rates of Reaction...........79
Reversible Reactions................................81
Mixed Practice Quizzes............................83

Topic 7 — Organic Chemistry
Crude Oil and Fractional Distillation 85
Alkanes and Cracking 87
Alkenes and their Reactions 89
Mixed Practice Quizzes 91
Addition Polymers 93
Alcohols 95
Carboxylic Acids and Esters 97
Condensation and Natural Polymers 99
Mixed Practice Quizzes 101

Topic 8 — Chemical Analysis
Purity, Formulations and Gas Tests 103
Paper Chromatography 105
Tests for Ions 107
Flame Tests and Spectroscopy 109
Mixed Practice Quizzes 111

Topic 9 — Chemistry of the Atmosphere
The Evolution of the Atmosphere 113
Greenhouse Gases & Climate Change .. 115
Carbon Footprints and Air Pollution 117
Mixed Practice Quizzes 119

Topic 10 — Using Resources
Materials 121
Metals and Corrosion 123
Resources & Life Cycle Assessments 125
Reuse and Recycling 127
Mixed Practice Quizzes 129
Treating Water 131
The Haber Process 133
NPK Fertilisers 135
Mixed Practice Quizzes 137

Required Practicals
Required Practicals 1 139
Required Practicals 2 141
Required Practicals 3 143
Required Practicals 4 145
Required Practicals 5 147
Mixed Practice Quizzes 149

Practical Skills
Apparatus and Techniques 151
Practical Techniques 153
Equipment and Heating Substances 155
Mixed Practice Quizzes 157

Published by CGP.
From original material by Richard Parsons.

Editors: Emily Forsberg, Rob Hayman, Sharon Keeley-Holden, George Wright
Contributor: Paddy Gannon

ISBN: 978 1 78908 494 8

With thanks to Emma Clayton, Mary Falkner and Glenn Rogers for the proofreading.
With thanks to Emily Smith for the copyright research.

Printed by Elanders Ltd, Newcastle upon Tyne.
Clipart from Corel®
Illustrations by: Sandy Gardner Artist, email sandy@sandygardner.co.uk

Text, design, layout and original illustrations © Coordination Group Publications Ltd (CGP) 2020
All rights reserved.

Photocopying this book is not permitted, even if you have a CLA licence.
Extra copies are available from CGP with next day delivery. • 0800 1712 712 • www.cgpbooks.co.uk

How to Use This Book

Every page in this book has a matching page in the GCSE Chemistry **Knowledge Organiser**. Before using this book, try to **memorise** everything on a Knowledge Organiser page. Then follow these **seven steps** to see how much knowledge you're able to retrieve...

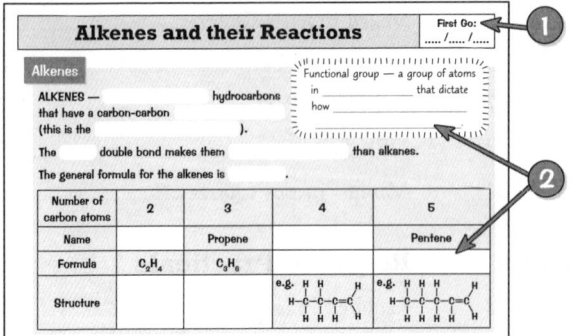

1. In this book, there are two versions of each page. Find the **'First Go'** of the page you've tried to memorise, and write the **date** at the top.

2. Use what you've learned from the Knowledge Organiser to **fill in** any dotted lines or white spaces. You may need to draw, complete or add labels to diagrams too.

3. Use the Knowledge Organiser to **check your work**. Use a **different coloured pen** to write in anything you missed or that wasn't quite right. This lets you see clearly what you **know** and what you **don't know**.

4. After doing the First Go page, **wait a few days**. This is important because **spacing out** your retrieval practice helps you to remember things better.

5. Now do the **Second Go** page. The Second Go page is harder — it has more things missing.

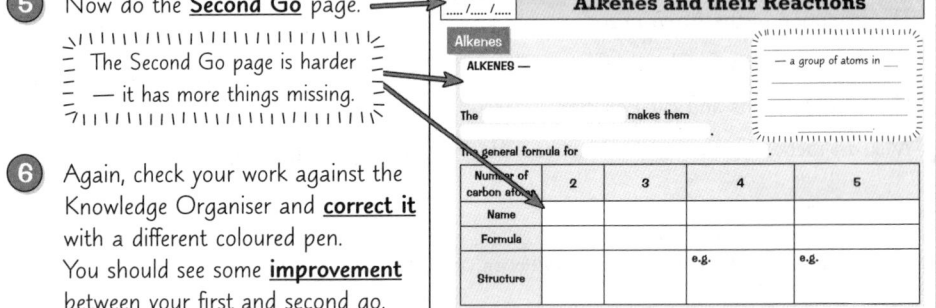

6. Again, check your work against the Knowledge Organiser and **correct it** with a different coloured pen. You should see some **improvement** between your first and second go.

7. **Wait** another few days, then try recreating the whole Knowledge Organiser page on a **blank piece of paper**. If you can do this, you'll know you've **really learned it**.

There are also **Mixed Practice Quizzes** dotted throughout the book:
- The quizzes come in sets of four. They test a mix of content from the previous few pages.
- Do each quiz on a different day — write the date you do each one at the top of the quiz.
- Tick the questions you get right and record your score in the box at the end.

The Scientific Method

First Go: ..... / ..... / .....

Developing Theories

Come up with ....
↓
....
↓
Evidence is peer-reviewed
↓
If all evidence backs up ...., it becomes an ....

HYPOTHESIS — a possible .... for ....

PEER REVIEW — when other scientists check results and explanations before ....

.... can still change over time e.g. the theory of atomic structure:

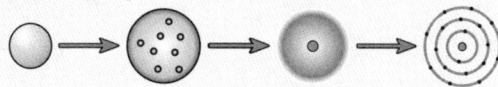

Models

REPRESENTATIONAL MODELS — a simplified .... of the ...., e.g. the different ways of showing covalent bonding:

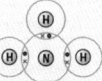 

Models help scientists explain .... and make ....

COMPUTATIONAL MODELS — computers are used to .... complex processes.

Issues in Science

.... can create four issues:

1. **Economic** — e.g. beneficial ...., like catalytic converters, may be too .... to use.
2. **Environmental** — e.g. .... could .... the natural environment.
3. **Social** — .... based on research can affect people, e.g. .... fossil fuels.
4. **Personal** — some decisions affect ...., e.g. a person may not want a wind farm being built ....

Media reports on scientific developments may be ...., inaccurate or ....

Hazard and Risk

HAZARD — something that could ....

RISK — the .... that a .... will cause harm.

Hazards associated with chemistry experiments include:

.... e.g. sulfuric acid

Faulty .... equipment

.... from Bunsen burners

The seriousness of the .... and the likelihood of .... both need consideration.

The Scientific Method

Second Go: ...../...../.....

Developing Theories

Come up with _____

↓

_____

↓

Evidence is _____

↓

If _____

HYPOTHESIS — _____

PEER REVIEW — _____

_____ can still change over time _____ e.g. _____ :

Models

REPRESENTATIONAL MODELS — a _____, e.g. the different ways of _____ :

_____ model

COMPUTATIONAL MODELS — _____

Models help scientists explain _____ .

Issues in Science

_____ can create four issues:

1. Economic — _____
2. _____
3. Social — _____
4. Personal — _____

_____ on scientific developments may be _____ .

Hazard and Risk

HAZARD — _____

RISK — _____

.... associated with chemistry experiments include:

_____

_____

_____

The _____ both need consideration.

Working Scientifically

Designing & Performing Experiments

First Go: ...../...../.....

Collecting Data

	Data should be...
REPEATABLE	Same person gets .... after repeating experiment using the .... and equipment.
....	Similar results can be achieved by .... or by using a different method or piece of ....
ACCURATE	Results are ....
....	All data is close to ....

Reliable data is .... and ....

↓

Valid results are .... and .... and answer the ....

Fair Tests

INDEPENDENT VARIABLE	Variable that you ....
.... VARIABLE	Variable that ....
.... VARIABLE	Variable that is ....
	An experiment kept under .... as .... without anything being done to it.
	An experiment where only .... changes, whilst all other variables are kept ....

.... are carried out when .... can't be controlled.

Four Things to Look Out For

1. **RANDOM ERRORS** — .... differences caused by things like .... in measuring.
2. **SYSTEMATIC ERRORS** — measurements that are wrong by .... each time.
3. **ZERO ERRORS** — systematic errors that are caused by using .... that isn't ....
4. **ANOMALOUS RESULTS** — results that .... with the rest of the data.

Anomalous results can be .... if you know ....

Processing Data

Calculate the .... — add together .... data values and .... number of values.

UNCERTAINTY — the amount by which a .... may differ from the ....

uncertainty = ───────────

.... value minus ....

In any calculation, you should round the answer to the .... number of significant figures (s.f.) given.

Working Scientifically

Designing & Performing Experiments

Second Go: ..... / ..... / .....

Collecting Data

	Data should be...	
	Same person gets	Reliable data
	Similar results can	
		Valid results

Fair Tests

.... can't be controlled.

INDEPENDENT VARIABLE —
— an experiment kept under the
— an experiment where

Four Things to Look Out For

1. **RANDOM ERRORS —**

2. **SYSTEMATIC ERRORS —**

3. **ZERO ERRORS —**

4. **ANOMALOUS RESULTS —**

   Anomalous results can be ....
   ....

Processing Data

———
add together
and divide by
.

UNCERTAINTY —

uncertainty =

In any calculation, ...
....

Working Scientifically

Presenting Data

First Go: ..... / ..... / .....

Bar Charts

Bar charts are used when independent variable is .... or ....

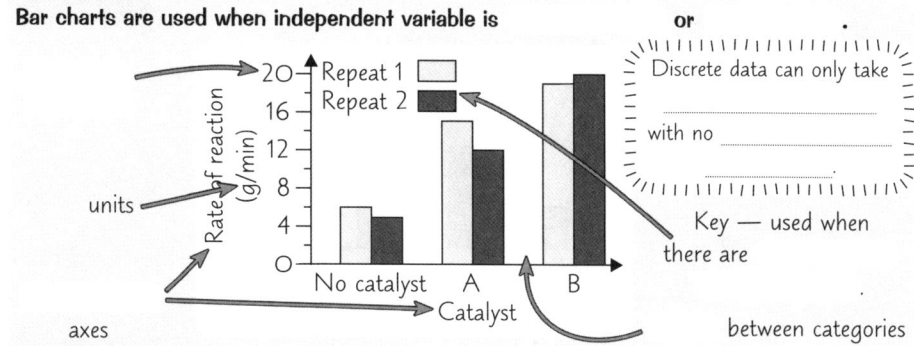

Discrete data can only take .... with no ....

Key — used when there are ....

units

axes

between categories

Plotting Graphs

Graphs are used when .... variables are ....

.... data — can take .... within a range.

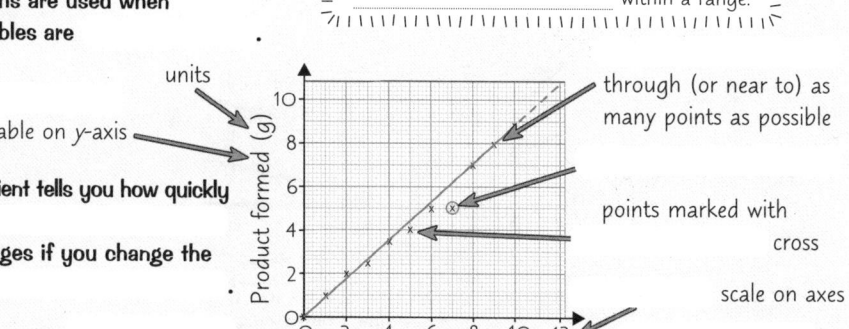

units

variable on y-axis

Gradient tells you how quickly .... changes if you change the ....

gradient = ————————

through (or near to) as many points as possible

points marked with .... cross

.... scale on axes

variable on x-axis

Three Types of Correlation Between Variables

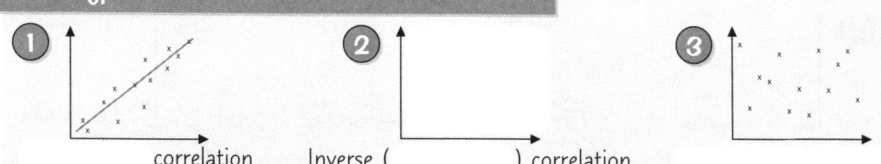

① .... correlation

② Inverse (............) correlation

③

Possible reasons for a correlation:

Chance — correlation might be ....

Third variable — .... the two variables.

Cause — if every other variable that .... the result is controlled, you can conclude that changing one variable .... in the other.

Working Scientifically

Presenting Data

Second Go: ..... / ..... / .....

Bar Charts

Bar charts are used when _____.

_____

_____

_____

Key — _____

_____

Plotting Graphs

_____ — can take _____.

Graphs are used when _____.

_____

_____

(or near to) _____

Gradient tells you _____

_____

_____

gradient = _____

variable on _____

Three Types of Correlation Between Variables

① _____

② _____

③ _____

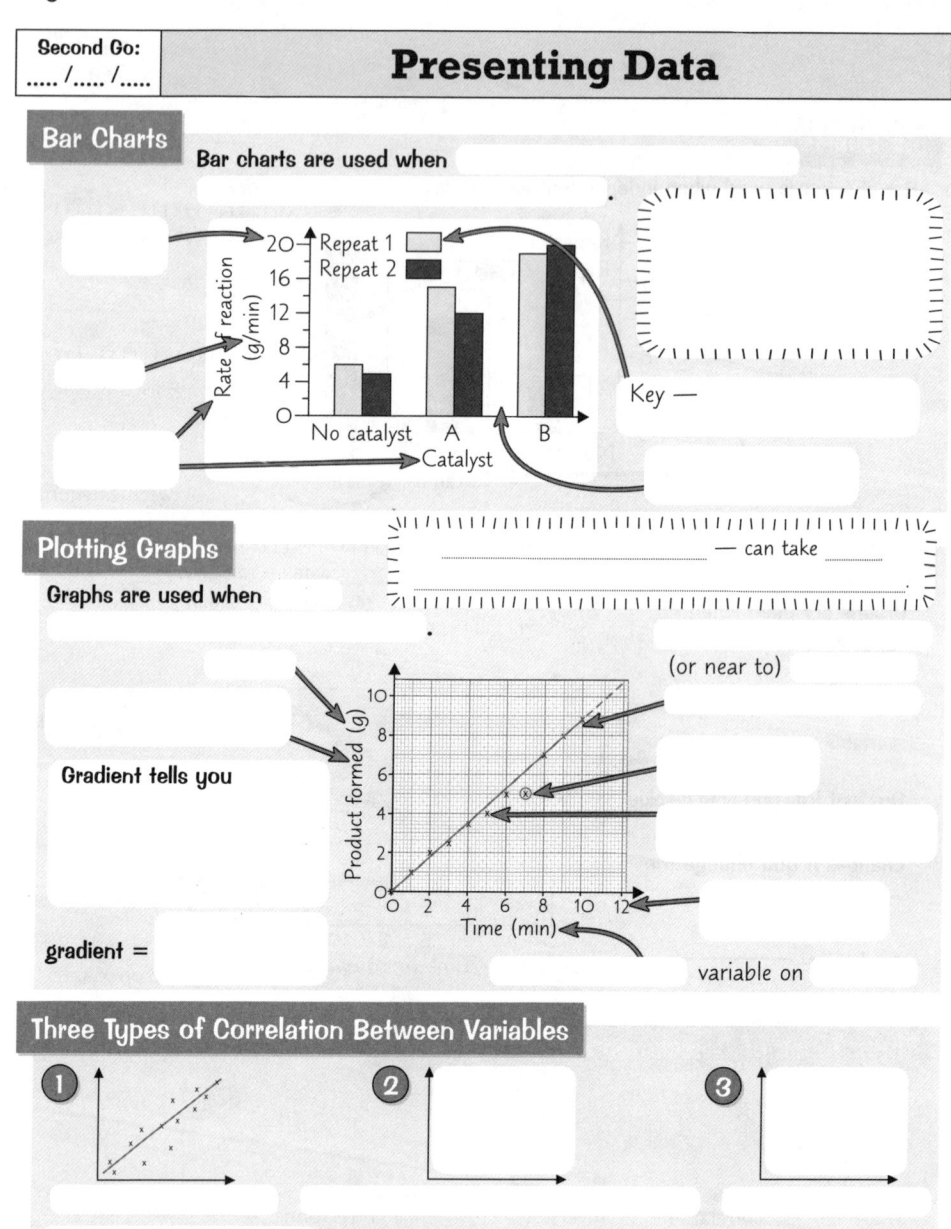

_____ for a correlation:

Chance — _____

Third variable — _____

Cause — _____

Working Scientifically

Conclusions, Evaluations and Units

First Go: ..... / ..... / .....

Conclusions

Draw conclusion by stating _____ between variables.

↓

Justify conclusion using _____ .

↓

Refer to _____ and state whether _____ .

> You can only draw a conclusion from _____ — you can't go any further than that.

Evaluations

EVALUATION — a _____ of the whole investigation.

	Things to consider
	• Validity of _____ • _____ variables
Results	• _____ , accuracy, _____ and _____ of results • Number of _____ taken • Level of _____ in the results
_____ results	• Causes of any _____ results

Repeating experiment with changes to improve the _____ will give you more _____ in your conclusions.

> You could make more predictions based on _____ , which you could test _____ .

S.I. Units

S.I. BASE UNITS — a set of _____ that _____ use.

Quantity	S.I. Unit
	kilogram ( )
length	( )
	second ( )
_____ of a substance	( )

Scaling Units

SCALING PREFIX — a word or _____ that goes _____ a unit to indicate a _____ .

Multiple of unit	Prefix
10^{12}	(T)
10^9	( )
	(M)
	kilo ( )
0.1	(d)
	centi ( )
0.001	( )
	micro ( )
10^{-9}	(n)

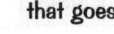

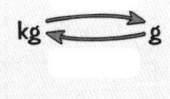

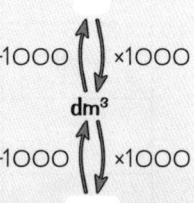

Working Scientifically

Conclusions, Evaluations and Units

Second Go: ...../...../.....

Conclusions

Draw conclusion by .... between ....

⬇

Justify conclusion ....

⬇

Refer to ....

> You can only draw a conclusion .... — you can't ....

Evaluations

EVALUATION — ....

	Things to consider

Repeating experiment

> You could .... based on your conclusion, ...

S.I. Units

S.I. BASE UNITS — ....

Quantity	S.I. Unit
	kilogram (kg)
length	

Scaling Units

SCALING PREFIX — ....

Multiple of unit	Prefix
	deci (d)
	centi (c)

.... ⇌ .... g

.... ⇅ dm³ ⇅ ....

Working Scientifically

Mixed Practice Quizzes

It's time for some quick quizzes to test you on p.3-10. Understanding how science works is super important, so give these quizzes a go and see how you get on.

Quiz 1 Date: ...... / ...... / ......

1) Give the equation used to find the gradient of a line on a graph.
2) When can an anomalous result in a data set be ignored?
3) Give two ways in which models can be useful to scientists.
4) Which term is given to a possible explanation for an observation?
5) What is an 'evaluation' of an investigation?
6) Give two examples of S.I. base units, and the quantities they are used to measure.
7) What two things must be considered when assessing a hazard?
8) When is it necessary to include a key in a bar chart?
9) How can you calculate the uncertainty of a mean value?
10) When might you need to carry out a control experiment?

Total:

Quiz 2 Date: ...... / ...... / ......

1) What is the range of a set of data?
2) Describe how to calculate the mean of a set of values.
3) When would you use a bar chart to represent data?
4) What can cause an accepted theory or model to change over time?
5) State the S.I. base unit for mass.
6) True or false? A conclusion cannot go beyond what the data shows.
7) What is a dependent variable?
8) Which type of model shows a real system as a simplified picture?
9) What is an anomalous result?
10) Give two types of issue that can result from scientific developments.

Total:

Working Scientifically

Mixed Practice Quizzes

Quiz 3   Date: ...... / ...... / ......

1) Give a hazard that is associated with chemistry experiments.
2) What makes an experiment a fair test?
3) What is meant by the term 'S.I. base unit'?
4) Give one issue associated with media reports on scientific developments.
5) What is meant by the term 'reliable data'?
6) What is peer review?
7) Give two reasons why a correlation between two variables does not always mean that changing one causes the change in the other.
8) True or false? The independent variable is shown on a graph's y-axis.
9) Give an example of an impact of a scientific development on individuals.
10) What is meant by the term 'uncertainty' when describing data?

Total:

Quiz 4   Date: ...... / ...... / ......

1) Give a suitable way to display data where both variables are continuous.
2) Give four examples of things to consider when evaluating an investigation.
3) True or false? A risk is something that could potentially cause harm.
4) What are random errors in an experiment?
5) Which scaling prefix indicates a multiplying factor of 0.001?
6) Give an example of an accepted theory that has changed over time.
7) Define the term 'systematic error'.
8) What is a control variable?
9) Define each of the following terms:
   a) Accurate data
   b) Precise data
   c) Valid results
10) How should a straight line of best fit be drawn on a graph?

Total:

Working Scientifically

Topic 1 — Atomic Structure and the Periodic Table

Atoms, Elements and Compounds

First Go: ...../...../.....

Atomic Structure

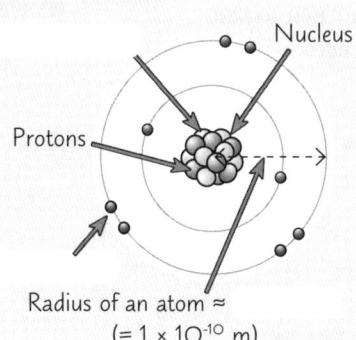

Nucleus
Protons
Radius of an atom ≈ (= 1×10^{-10} m)
≈ 1×10^{-14} m

Atoms have no overall charge (number of .... = number of ....).

Particle	Relative mass	Relative charge
Proton		+1
Neutron	1	
	Very small	−1

Nuclear Symbols

NUCLEAR SYMBOL — used to describe atoms:

.... = total number of protons and neutrons in an atom

$^{23}_{11}$Na

Atomic number = number of .... in an atom

Elements

There are about .... different elements.

ELEMENTS — substances made up of atoms with the same ....

.... of an element — atoms with .... number of protons but .... numbers of neutrons.

.... (A_r) — the average mass number for an element:

$$A_r = \frac{\text{sum of (} .... \times \text{ isotope mass number)}}{\text{total abundance of all isotopes}}$$

Compounds

COMPOUND — substance formed from .... elements in fixed proportions.

At least one new substance is made in a chemical reaction. You can usually ....

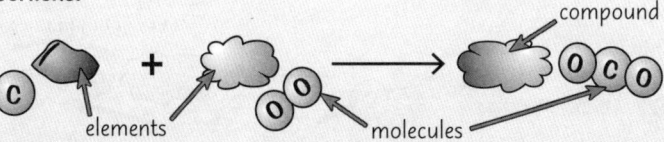

elements → molecules → compound

MOLECULE — particle containing two or more non-metal atoms bonded ....

Molecules can be .... (if they only have .... of atom) or compounds.

Topic 1 — Atomic Structure and the Periodic Table

Atoms, Elements and Compounds

Second Go: ..... / ..... / .....

Atomic Structure

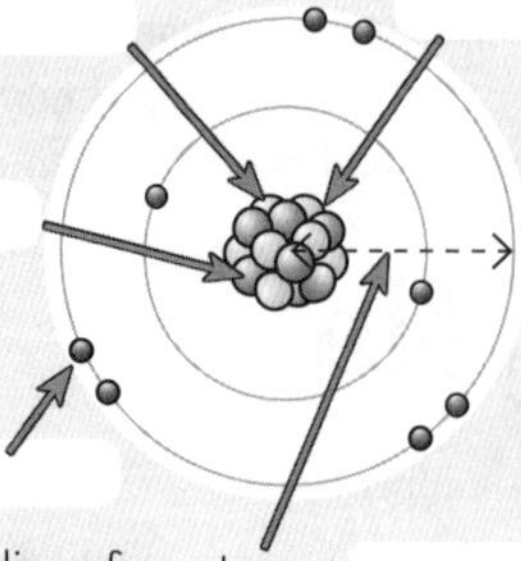

Radius of an atom ≈ ....

.... ≈

Atoms have ....

		+1
Neutron		
	Very small	

Nuclear Symbols

NUCLEAR SYMBOL — used to .... :

.... = ...

$^{23}_{11}Na$

.... = ...

Elements

There are about .... different elements.

ELEMENTS —

.... (A_r) — the average .... :

A_r =

Compounds

COMPOUND —

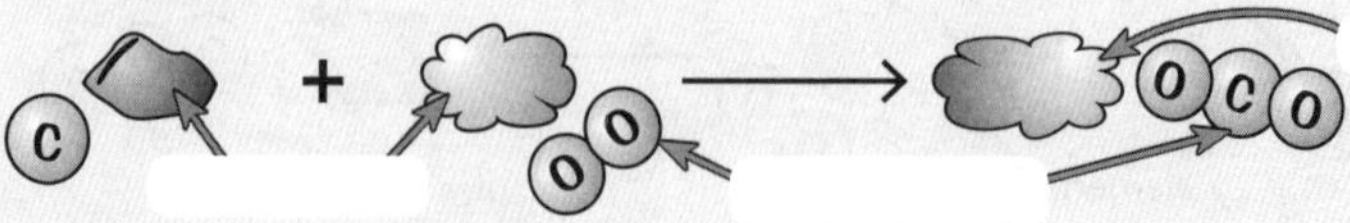

MOLECULE — particle containing ....

Topic 1 — Atomic Structure and the Periodic Table

Equations, Mixtures & Chromatography

First Go: ..... /..... /.....

Chemical Formulas and Equations

Chemical formula — shows the .... in a compound.

E.g. CO_2 ⟵ .... for every carbon atom

Chemical equation — shows the .... in a reaction.

               Products

       methane + oxygen → .... + water

Symbol equation: .... + $2O_2$ → CO_2 + ...

There must be .... of each atom on each side so the equation is ....

The .... in front of the .... tell you how many units of that .... there are.

Mixtures

MIXTURES — substances made up of different .... or compounds that .... to each other.

E.g. air is a mixture.

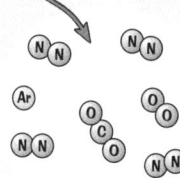

The .... of a substance aren't affected by being ....

```
Mixtures can be separated by ...............
............... — these don't involve
............... or form ...............
```

Paper Chromatography

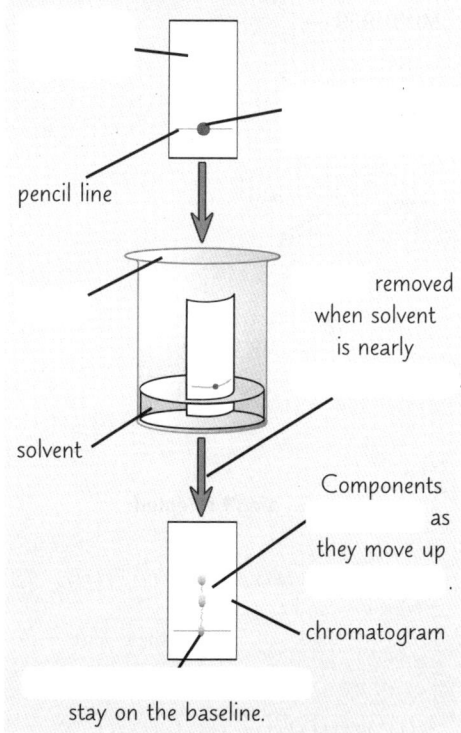

pencil line

removed when solvent is nearly ....

solvent

Components .... as they move up ....

chromatogram

stay on the baseline.

Topic 1 — Atomic Structure and the Periodic Table

Second Go: ...../...../..... Equations, Mixtures & Chromatography

Chemical Formulas and Equations

Chemical formula —

E.g. CO_2

Chemical equation — .

methane + → + water

+ $2O_2$ → CO_2 +

There must be the

Mixtures

MIXTURES —

E.g. air is a mixture.

The aren't affected .

Mixtures can be — these don't

Paper Chromatography

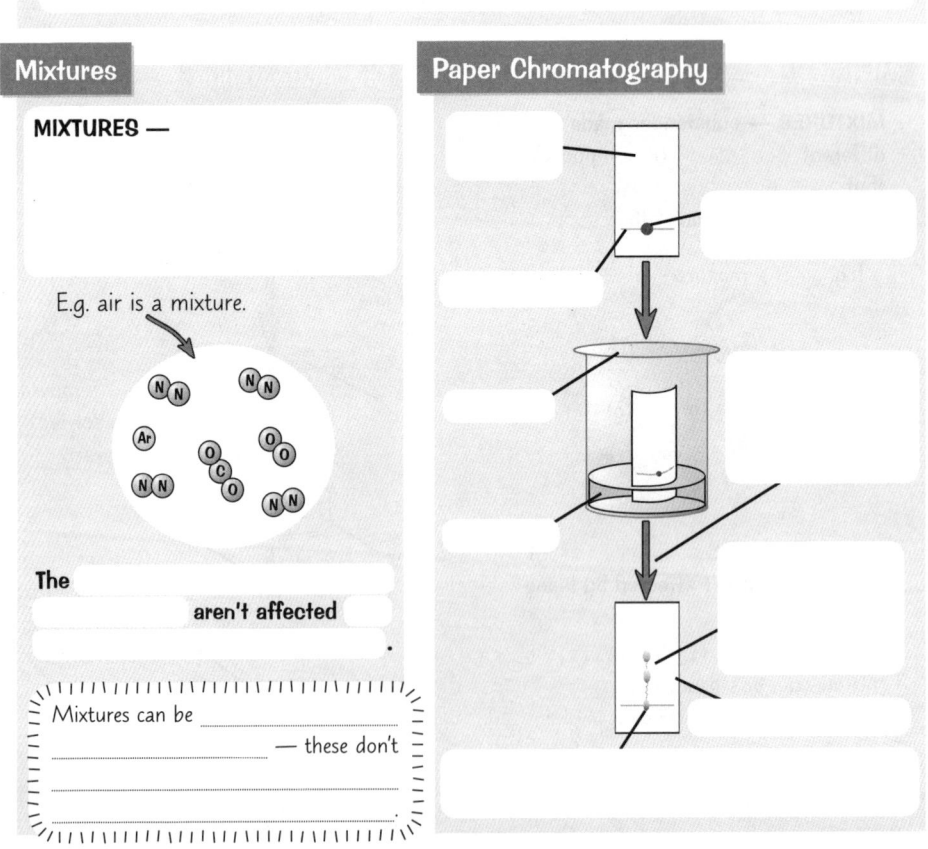

Topic 1 — Atomic Structure and the Periodic Table

More Separation Techniques

First Go: ..... / ..... / .....

Filtration

FILTRATION — separates _____ from liquids and _____.

It can be used to separate out _____, or _____ by removing _____.

Solid left in the _____.

Evaporation

EVAPORATION — separates _____ from solution.

evaporating dish

Slowly _____ solution.

and dry out as solvent _____.

Evaporation is _____, but can't be used if the _____ when heated.

Crystallisation

CRYSTALLISATION — also separates _____ from solution.

Heat solution, but _____ when _____ start to form.

↓

_____ form as solution cools.

↓

Filter out _____ and leave to _____.

Use crystallisation for salts that _____, or if you want _____.

Two Types of Distillation

1 Simple distillation

The part with the _____ evaporates first.

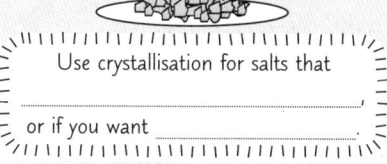

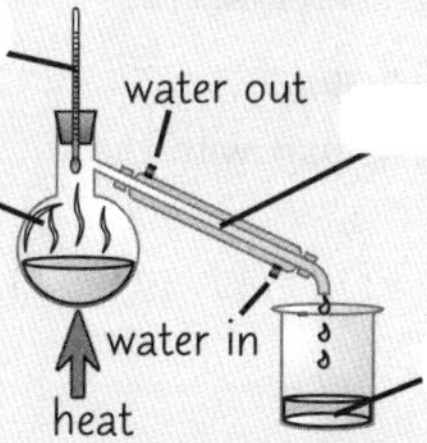

water out

water in

heat

_____ and condenses.

_____ can't separate liquids with _____, but fractional distillation can.

2 Fractional distillation

thermometer

Liquids reach the _____ when the temperature at the top _____.

fractionating column filled with _____

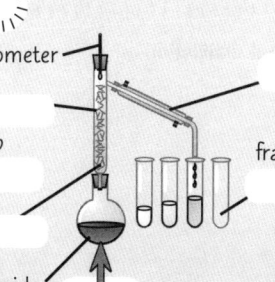

fractions collected

mixture of liquids

Topic 1 — Atomic Structure and the Periodic Table

More Separation Techniques

Second Go: ..... / ..... / .....

Filtration

FILTRATION —

It can be used

Evaporation

EVAPORATION —

solution.

Evaporation is _____, but can't be used if the _____.

Crystallisation

CRYSTALLISATION —

Use crystallisation for _____, or if you _____.

Two Types of Distillation

1) Simple distillation
The part with the

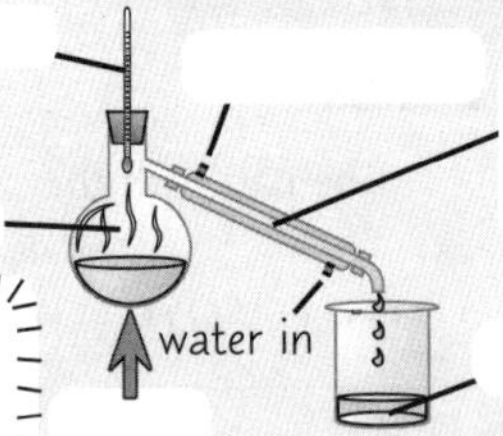

2) Fractional distillation

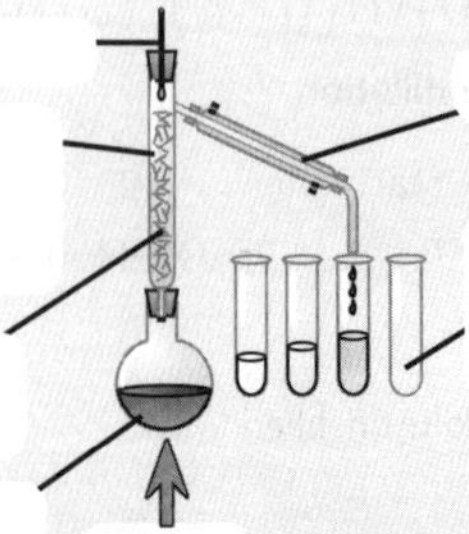

Atomic and Electronic Structure

First Go: ..... / ..... / .....

The History of the Atom

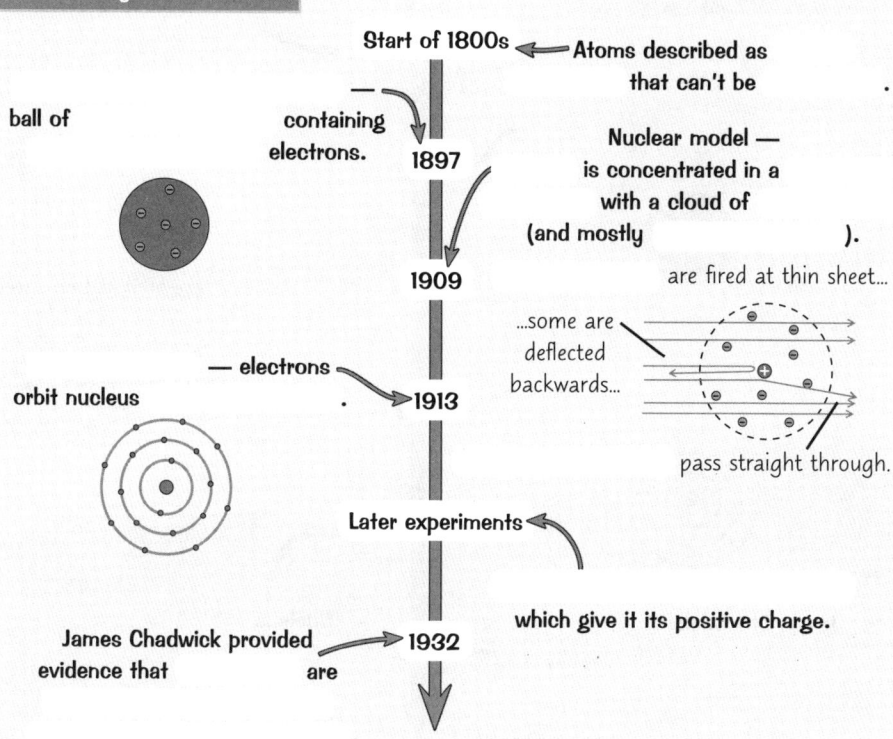

Start of 1800s ← Atoms described as _____ that can't be _____.

ball of _____ containing electrons.

1897

Nuclear model — _____ is concentrated in a _____ with a cloud of _____ (and mostly _____).

1909

_____ are fired at thin sheet...

...some are deflected backwards...

..._____ pass straight through.

— electrons _____ orbit nucleus

1913

Later experiments ←

James Chadwick provided evidence that _____ are _____

1932

which give it its positive charge.

Electronic Structure

Electrons occupy _____ — sometimes called energy _____.

Electrons _____ one, starting with the _____ before occupying a new _____.

Shell	.... allowed in shell
1	2
2	
	8

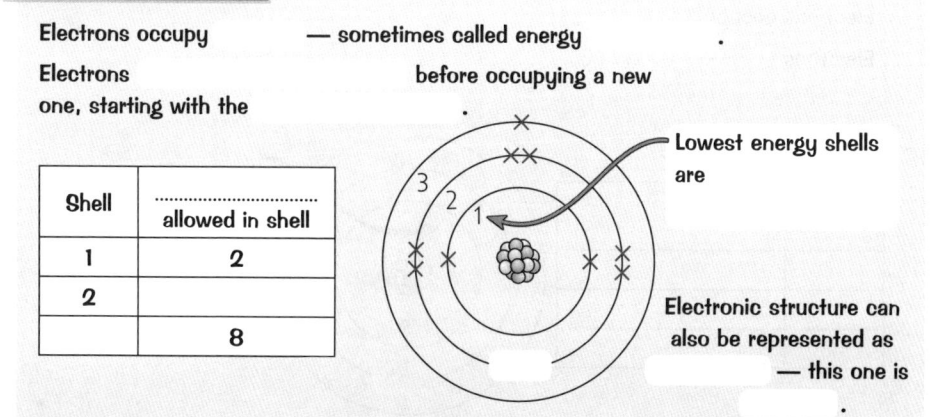

Lowest energy shells are _____

Electronic structure can also be represented as _____ — this one is _____.

Topic 1 — Atomic Structure and the Periodic Table

Atomic and Electronic Structure

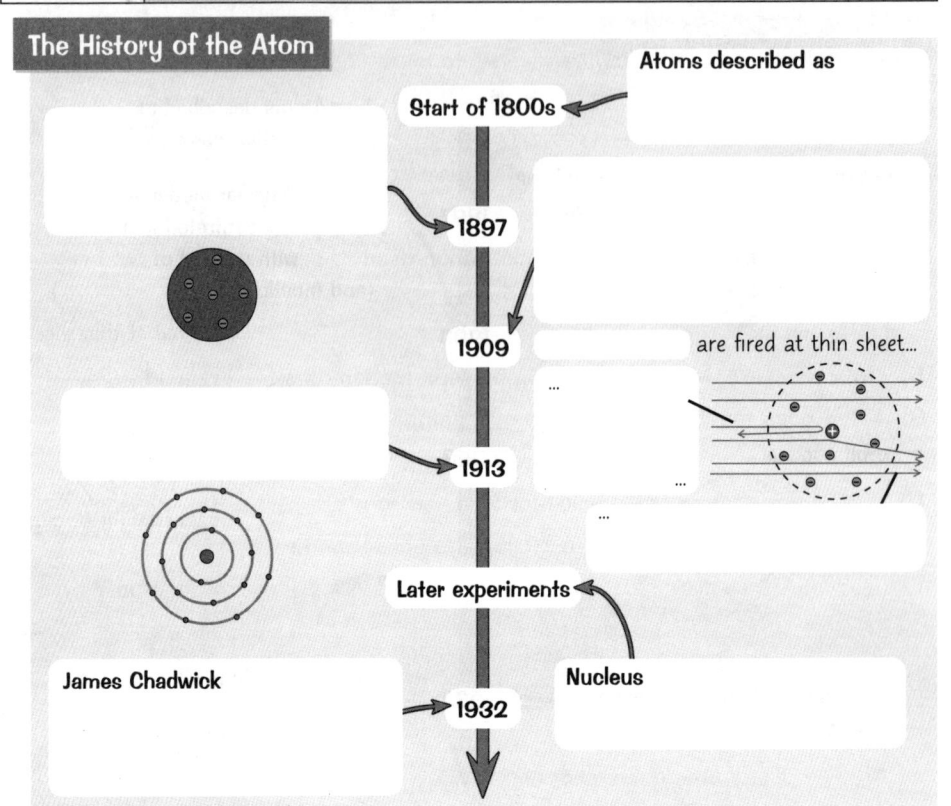

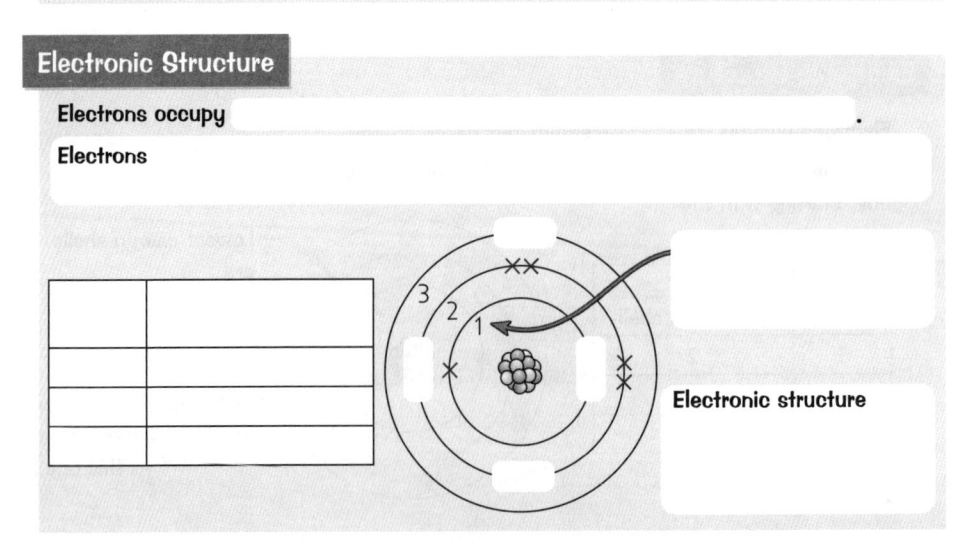

Second Go: ..../..../....

The History of the Atom

Atoms described as

Start of 1800s

1897

1909

1913

...are fired at thin sheet...

Later experiments

James Chadwick

Nucleus

1932

Electronic Structure

Electrons occupy _____ .

Electrons

Electronic structure

Topic 1 — Atomic Structure and the Periodic Table

Mixed Practice Quizzes

You've made it through the first half of Topic 1. Now have a go at these four quizzes based on p.13-20 and remember to mark yourself when you're done.

Quiz 1 — Date: ...... / ...... / ......

1) What is the approximate radius of a nucleus?
2) What is the overall charge of an atom?
3) What type of mixture is simple distillation used to separate?
4) Which part of an atom's nuclear symbol shows the number of protons in an atom of that element?
5) True or false? Mixtures can only be separated by chemical reactions.
6) What does the chemical formula of a compound show?
7) What type of mixture can crystallisation be used to separate?
8) Which scientist provided evidence that neutrons are part of the nucleus?
9) True or false? There are about 100 different elements.
10) How many electrons are allowed in the lowest energy shell of an atom?

Total:

Quiz 2 — Date: ...... / ...... / ......

1) True or false? The nucleus of an atom is negatively charged.
2) What happens to the majority of α-particles when they're fired at a thin sheet of atoms?
3) How is the relative atomic mass (A_r) of an element calculated?
4) Define the term 'mixture'.
5) What is the approximate radius of an atom?
6) What is the final step when crystallising a salt?
7) True or false? Each of the particles that make up an atom have the same relative mass.
8) Which part of a mixture of liquids will evaporate first in simple distillation?
9) Where are the electron shells with the lowest energy in an atom?
10) What does the mass number tell you about an atom?

Total:

Topic 1 — Atomic Structure and the Periodic Table

Mixed Practice Quizzes

Quiz 3   Date: ...... / ...... / ......

1) Where does the nuclear model say the mass of an atom is concentrated?
2) What is the relative charge of an electron?
3) Define what is meant by the term 'compound'.
4) What is shown by the large numbers in front of chemical formulas in chemical equations?
5) When should the filter paper be removed from the solvent when carrying out paper chromatography?
6) What is the relative mass of a neutron?
7) Which technique could you use to separate an insoluble solid from a solution?
8) Describe the 'plum pudding' model of the atom.
9) True or false? Atomic number is equal to the number of neutrons in that atom.
10) What did the Bohr model suggest about the structure of the atom?

Total:

Quiz 4   Date: ...... / ...... / ......

1) What name is given to the positively charged particles in an atom?
2) How many electrons are allowed in the second electron shell of an atom?
3) What is the mass of an electron relative to the mass of a proton?
4) What is meant by the term 'isotope'?
5) True or false? Molecules are particles containing a metal atom and a non-metal atom.
6) Give two ways of showing the overall change in a chemical reaction.
7) How many oxygen atoms are present in one molecule of CO_2?
8) What happens to the insoluble components of a mixture being separated by chromatography?
9) Which type of distillation can be used to separate compounds with similar boiling points?
10) Which atomic model shows electrons orbiting the nucleus in fixed shells?

Total:

Topic 1 — Atomic Structure and the Periodic Table

The Periodic Table

First Go:
...../...../.....

Mendeleev's Table

Before atomic structure was discovered, _____
was used to order _____.

In Mendeleev's Table of Elements, the elements were _____
using _____, instead of strictly following _____.

Mendeleev had to _____
in the table to _____ which fitted into _____
_____ the gaps were _____.

```
H
Li Be                          B  C  N  O  F
Na Mg                          Al Si P  S  Cl
K  Ca *  Ti V  Cr Mn Fe Co Ni Cu Zn *  *  As Se Br
Rb Sr Y  Zr Nb Mo *  Ru Rh Pd Ag Cd In Sn Sb Te I
Cs Ba *  *  Ta W  *  Os Ir Pt Au Hg Tl Pb Bi
```

Mendeleev _____   Discovery of _____   explained
_____ in places where ordering by _____   why _____   cannot be strictly
_____ didn't fit the pattern.   ordered by _____.

The Modern Periodic Table

The _____ are ordered by _____.

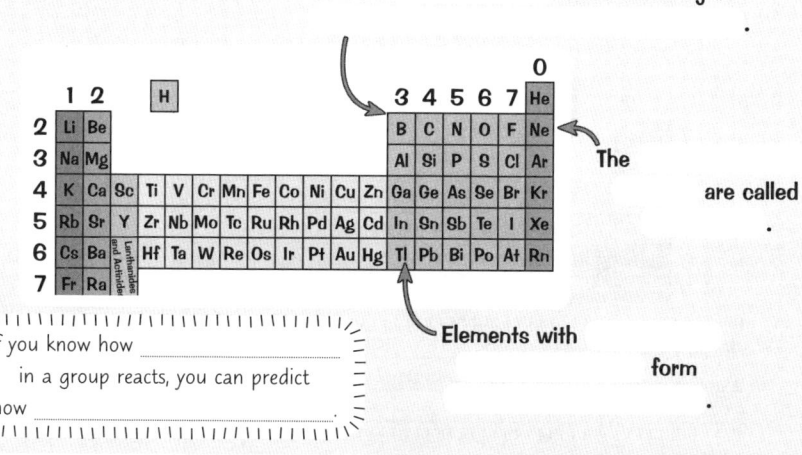

The _____ are called _____.

Elements with _____ form _____.

If you know how _____
 in a group reacts, you can predict
 how _____

_____ tells you the electronic structure:

Group number = the number of electrons in the _____.

_____ = the number of shells with electrons in.

Topic 1 — Atomic Structure and the Periodic Table

The Periodic Table

Second Go: ...../...../.....

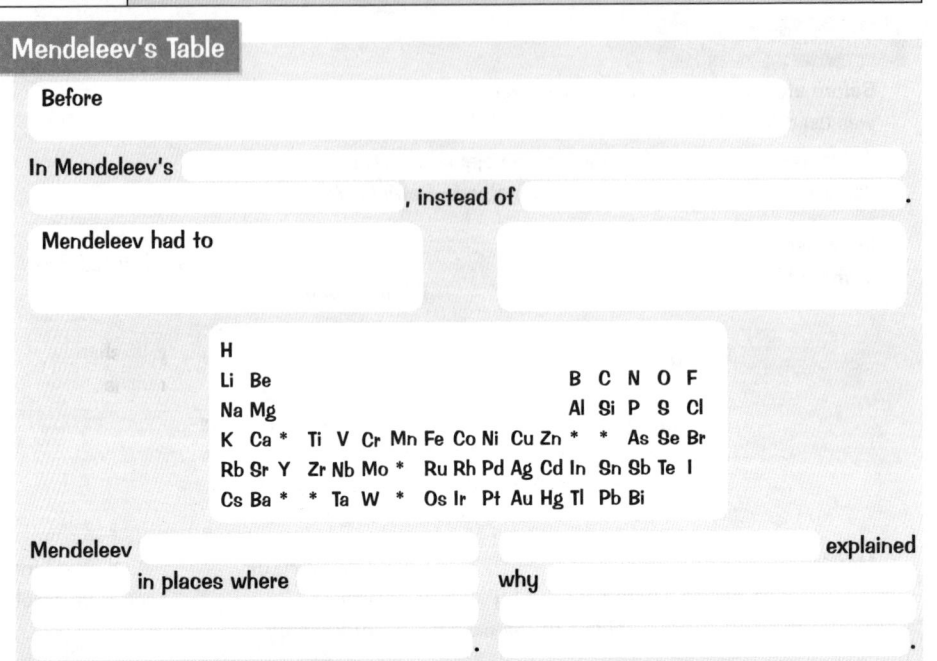

Mendeleev's Table

Before

In Mendeleev's _____ , instead of _____ .

Mendeleev had to

```
H
Li Be                                          B  C  N  O  F
Na Mg                                          Al Si P  S  Cl
K  Ca *  Ti V  Cr Mn Fe Co Ni Cu Zn *  *  As Se Br
Rb Sr Y  Zr Nb Mo *  Ru Rh Pd Ag Cd In Sn Sb Te I
Cs Ba *  *  Ta W  *  Os Ir Pt Au Hg Tl Pb Bi
```

Mendeleev _____ explained

in places where _____ why _____ .

The Modern Periodic Table

If you know how _____ in a group reacts, _____

_____ tells you the _____ :

_____ = _____

_____ = _____

Topic 1 — Atomic Structure and the Periodic Table

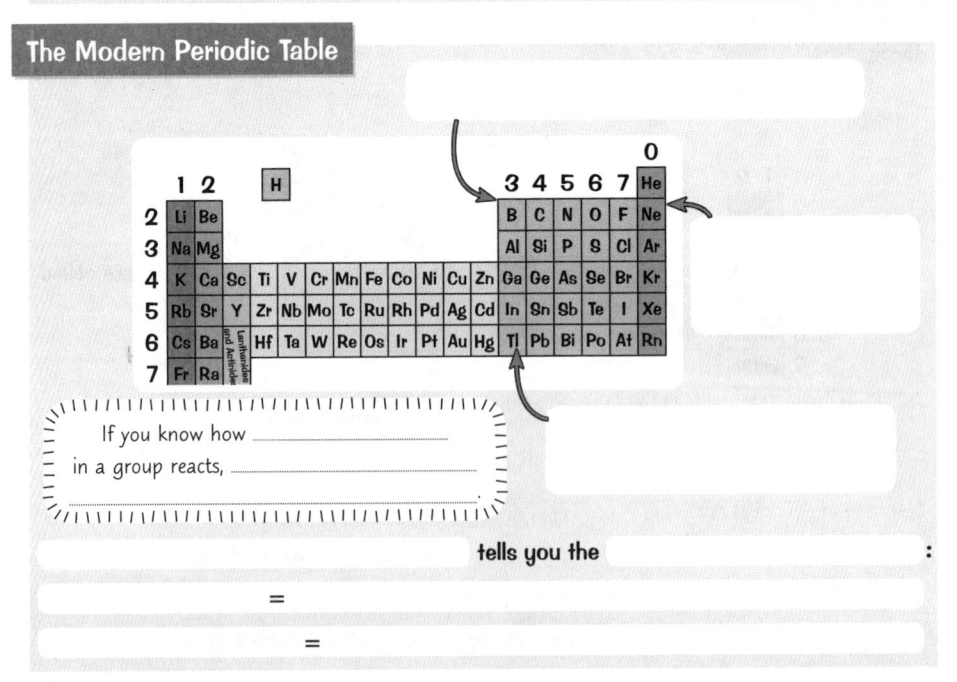

Metals and Non-Metals

First Go: ...../...../......

Reactivity of Metals and Non-Metals

METALS — elements that _____ when they react.

_____ — elements that _____.

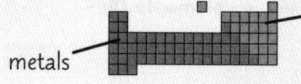

metals

Atoms tend to react to form _____.

	Metals	Non-metals
Get a full outer shell by...		...gaining or sharing electrons
More reactive when they...	...lose electrons more easily	
More reactive towards...	.... of the periodic table	...the top right of the periodic table

Properties of Metals and Non-Metals

Appearance			Dull
Strength			Brittle
Melting and boiling points		High	Low
Conductivity		Good .... conductors	.... conductors

These are general properties — they're not true for every metal or non-metal.

Transition Metals

TRANSITION METALS — metals in _____.

Examples of transition metals:
Cr _____ Fe _____ Co _____ Cu

Transition metals have _____, _____, but are different in three main ways:

1. They have _____.
   e.g. Fe^{2+} _____

2. They form _____ compounds.

3. They can be good _____.

Topic 1 — Atomic Structure and the Periodic Table

Metals and Non-Metals

Second Go: ..... / ..... / .....

Reactivity of Metals and Non-Metals

METALS — .... — elements that ....

	Metals	Non-metals
Get a .... by...		
More	...lose electrons more easily	
More	.... of the periodic table	...the top right of the periodic table

Properties of Metals and Non-Metals

Appearance		
Strength		
Melting and boiling points		
Conductivity		

These are ....
— they're not true for ....
....

Transition Metals

....
....

Examples of transition metals:
....

Transition metals have ....

① They have ....
   e.g. ....

② ....

③ ....

Topic 1 — Atomic Structure and the Periodic Table

Group 1 and Group 0 Elements

First Go: ..... / ..... / .....

Trends in Group 1

_____ — common name for the _____ .

As you go .... Group 1:	
Reactivity	increases
Melting and boiling points	....
Relative	increases

$^{7}_{3}$Li
$^{23}_{11}$Na
$^{39}_{19}$K
$^{85}_{37}$Rb
$^{133}_{55}$Cs
$^{223}_{87}$Fr

Properties of Group 1 Metals

Group 1 metals have different properties from most other metals:

They're much _____ .

They're _____ and softer.

They have _____ melting points.

> Compared to _____ , Group 1 metals have a _____ _____ , are more reactive and are less dense, _____ and hard.

Reactions of Group 1 Elements

The Group 1 elements only have — _____ to lose it so they readily form _____ .

They react with a range of substances to form _____ :

metal + ... → metal hydroxide + hydrogen

metal + chlorine → ....

metal + ... → ....

> As reactivity increases .... , _____ the reaction with water becomes more _____ .

Group 0 Elements

GROUP 0 ELEMENTS — non-metals with _____ .

Their _____ is stable so they are _____ .

All Group 0 elements are _____ at room temperature.

> These elements are also known as the _____ .

As you go DOWN Group 0, the boiling point ....

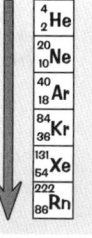

$^{4}_{2}$He
$^{20}_{10}$Ne
$^{40}_{18}$Ar
$^{84}_{36}$Kr
$^{131}_{54}$Xe
$^{222}_{86}$Rn

Topic 1 — Atomic Structure and the Periodic Table

Group 1 and Group 0 Elements

Second Go: ..... / ..... / .....

Trends in Group 1

_____ — common name for the _____ .

As you go .... :		$^{7}_{3}$Li
		$^{23}_{11}$Na
		$^{39}_{19}$K
		$^{85}_{37}$Rb
		$^{133}_{55}$Cs
		$^{223}_{87}$Fr

Properties of Group 1 Metals

_____

They're much _____ .
They're less _____ .
They have lower _____ .

_____ , Group 1 metals have a _____ , are _____ and are _____ .

Reactions of Group 1 Elements

The Group 1 elements _____

They react with _____

metal + ... → .... + ...

metal + ... → ....

metal + ... → ....

Group 0 Elements

GROUP 0 ELEMENTS — _____ .

Their _____

All Group 0 elements _____

These elements are also known as the _____ .

As you _____ .
_____ .

| $^{4}_{2}$He |
| $^{20}_{10}$Ne |
| $^{40}_{18}$Ar |
| $^{84}_{36}$Kr |
| $^{131}_{54}$Xe |
| $^{222}_{86}$Rn |

Topic 1 — Atomic Structure and the Periodic Table

Group 7 Elements

First Go: ..... / ..... / .....

Trends in Group 7

GROUP 7 ELEMENTS — non-metals known as _____.

Halogen		Chlorine	Bromine	
Appearance	yellow gas	.... gas	volatile red-brown	dark grey solid or purple vapour

As you go .... Group 7:	
	decreases
Melting and boiling points	
	increases

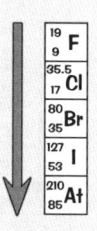

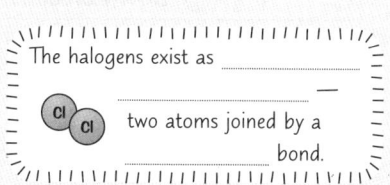

The halogens exist as _____ — two atoms joined by a _____ bond.

Reactions of Group 7 Elements

Halogens have _____ — they need _____ to be filled.

They can react to fill their outer shell in two ways:

1 _____

Halogens form _____ with other _____ to form molecular compounds.

2 _____

- Halogens form _____ when they react with _____.
- As they gain _____, they form 1− ions called _____.

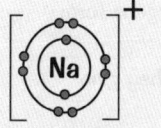 

_____ halogens can displace _____ ones.

E.g. _____ + 2KBr$_{(aq)}$ → _____ + 2KCl$_{(aq)}$ ← _____ is more reactive than _____ so displaces it from the salt.

Topic 1 — Atomic Structure and the Periodic Table

Group 7 Elements

Second Go: ...../...../......

Trends in Group 7

GROUP 7 ELEMENTS — _____.

Halogen			Bromine	
Appearance	yellow gas			

As you go DOWN Group 7:	

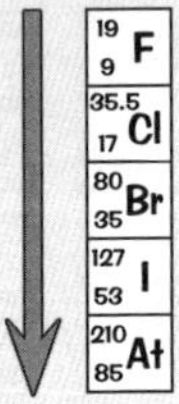

The _____ exist as _____ — _____ joined by a _____.

Reactions of Group 7 Elements

Halogens have _____

They can _____ :

 Halogens form _____

- Halogens form _____
- As they gain _____

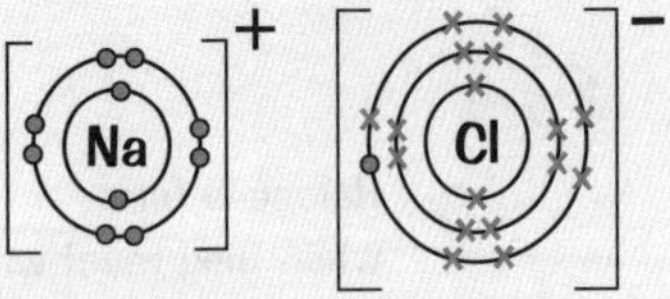

_____

E.g. _____ + 2 _____(aq) → _____ + 2 _____(aq)   ← _____ is more reactive than _____.

Topic 1 — Atomic Structure and the Periodic Table

Mixed Practice Quizzes

Now, a good chemist likes to do a quiz periodically. Helpfully, here are four practice ones covering the different properties of elements from p.23-30.

Quiz 1 Date: ...... / ...... / ......

1) Describe the typical appearance of a metal.
2) True or false? Group 1 metals are denser than most other metals.
3) Describe the appearance of fluorine gas.
4) How are the elements ordered in the modern periodic table?
5) How does reactivity change as you go down Group 1?
6) What does an element's period number tell you about its electronic structure?
7) What are the Group 0 elements also known as?
8) How many atoms make up a halogen molecule?
9) What is the charge on the ions formed by atoms of Group 1 elements?
10) Which discovery explained why elements cannot be strictly ordered by atomic weight to fit in the Periodic Table?

Total:

Quiz 2 Date: ...... / ...... / ......

1) How many electrons are in the outer shell of a halogen atom?
2) What type of elements react to form positive ions?
3) How do the melting points of Group 1 metals compare to the melting points of transition metals?
4) Which halogen is a dark grey solid?
5) Describe the electrical and thermal conductivity of non-metals.
6) How were elements ordered before the discovery of atomic structure?
7) Give one way that halogens can react to fill their outer electron shell.
8) Why did Mendeleev leave gaps in his Table of Elements?
9) What is an alternative name for the Group 1 metals?
10) What type of compound is formed when a metal reacts with a halogen?

Total:

Topic 1 — Atomic Structure and the Periodic Table

Mixed Practice Quizzes

Quiz 3 Date: ...... / ...... / ......

1) Give two general properties of non-metals.
2) True or false? Metals are better electrical conductors than most non-metals.
3) Which set of metals make good catalysts?
4) How does the relative molecular mass of the elements change as you go down Group 7?
5) Give one thing that is unusual about transition metal ions.
6) True or false? Non-metals normally react by gaining or sharing electrons.
7) Describe the reactivity of the Group 0 elements.
8) True or false? Non-metals typically have high boiling points.
9) Do the Group 0 elements exist as solids, liquids or gases at room temperature?
10) What is shown by an element's group number?

Total:

Quiz 4 Date: ...... / ...... / ......

1) How did Mendeleev group elements in his Table of Elements?
2) State two ways that transition metals differ from other metals.
3) What is produced when a Group 1 metal reacts with water?
4) Where in the periodic table would you find the most reactive metals?
5) Compare the typical strengths of metals and non-metals.
6) Give the product of the reaction between an alkali metal and oxygen.
7) What happens to the boiling point of the Group 0 elements as you go down the group?
8) True or false? Bromine can displace chlorine from an aqueous solution of its salt.
9) Why are the noble gases unreactive?
10) What name is given to the horizontal rows of the periodic table?

Total:

Topic 1 — Atomic Structure and the Periodic Table

Topic 2 — Bonding, Structure and Properties of Matter

Ions and Ionic Bonding

First Go: ..... /..... /.....

Ion Formation

IONS — _____ made when _____ are transferred.

	Electron transfer	Group	Charge of ion
metals	_____ electrons (form _____ ions)	2	
non-metals	_____ electrons (form _____ ions)	6	
			1−

The _____ formed by _____ have the electronic structure of _____.

Ionic Bonding

IONIC BONDING — _____
between _____ ions. Ionic bonding occurs between _____ metal ions and _____ non-metal ions.

Sodium Chloride

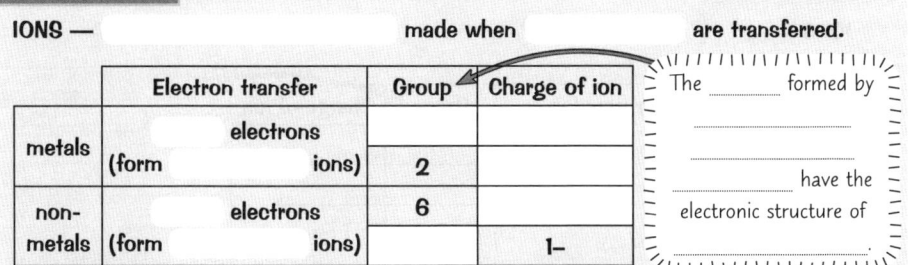

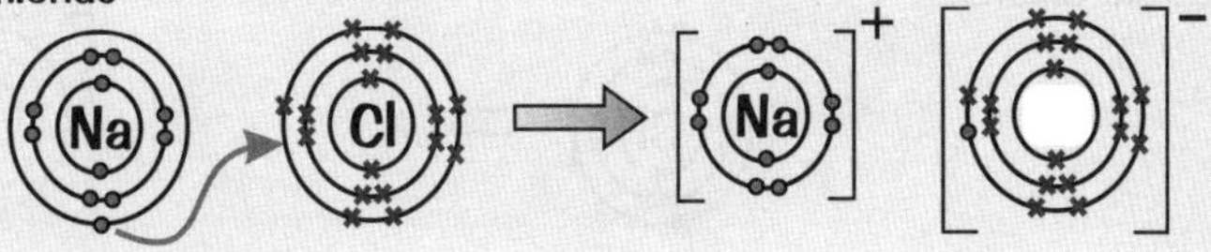

Na
2, 8, 1

_____ atom   chlorine atom   sodium ion   2, 8, 8

_____ diagrams don't show compound _____ or the size and _____ of ions.

Three Properties of Ionic Compounds

1 Giant ionic lattice structure — _____ of attraction between oppositely charged ions act _____.

2 High _____ points — lots of energy needed to _____.

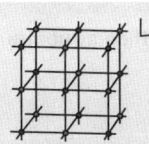

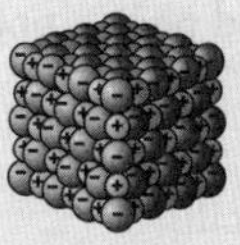

3 Conduct electricity only when _____ — ions free to move and _____.

Limitations:
• Model not _____
• In reality, no _____ between ions

Limitation: can only see _____ of compound.

_____ of ionic compounds can be worked out from diagrams.

Ions and Ionic Bonding

Second Go: ..... / ..... / .....

Ion Formation

IONS —

	Electron transfer	Group	Charge of ion
metals			
non-metals			

The .... have the ....

Ionic Bonding

IONIC BONDING — .... Ionic bonding occurs between ....

Sodium Chloride

[Cl 2,8,7] → [Cl 2,8,8]⁻
Cl⁻
2, 8, 8
chloride ion

don't show ....

Three Properties of Ionic Compounds

1 Giant ionic lattice structure —

Limitations:
•
•

2 High melting and boiling points —

Limitation:

3 Conduct electricity

.... can be worked out ....

Topic 2 — Bonding, Structure and Properties of Matter

Covalent Bonding & Simple Molecules

First Go: ...../...../.....

Covalent Bonding

COVALENT BOND — a _____ pair of electrons between two _____.
Covalent bonding happens in non-metal _____ and in non-metal _____.

Molecular formulas show you _____ of each element are in _____. NH_3

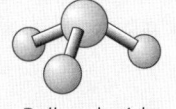

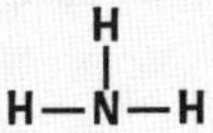

Dot and cross diagrams don't show _____ of atoms or their _____ in space.

Ball and stick diagrams don't show the electrons in _____ come from.

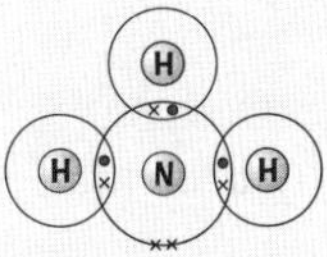

Displayed formula — doesn't show _____

H
|
H—N—H

Simple Molecular Substances

Covalent bonds between _____ are _____.
Forces between _____ are _____.

Elements

(H_2) | Oxygen | Nitrogen 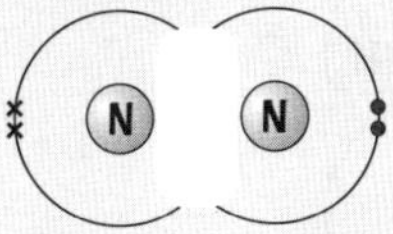 | Chlorine (Cl_2)

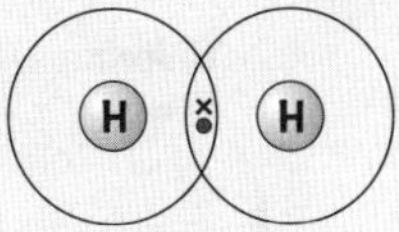

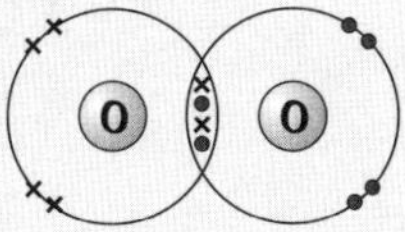

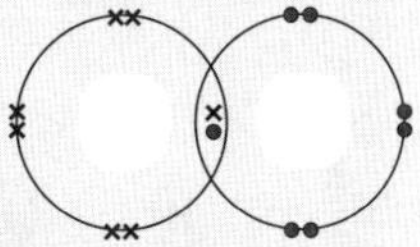

Compounds

Hydrogen Chloride (HCl) | Water | Ammonia | Methane

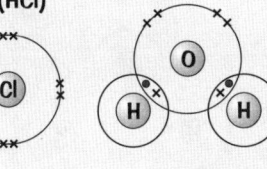

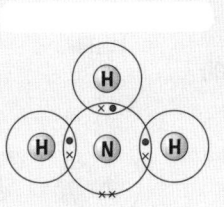

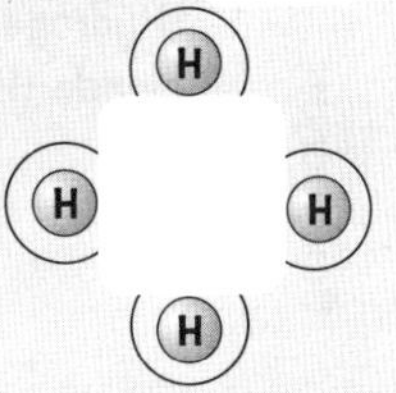

Two Properties of Simple Molecular Substances

1. Low melting and boiling points
   — mostly _____ at _____.

2. Don't conduct electricity
   — there are _____ particles to _____.

As molecules get _____, less energy is needed to _____ between them.

Topic 2 — Bonding, Structure and Properties of Matter

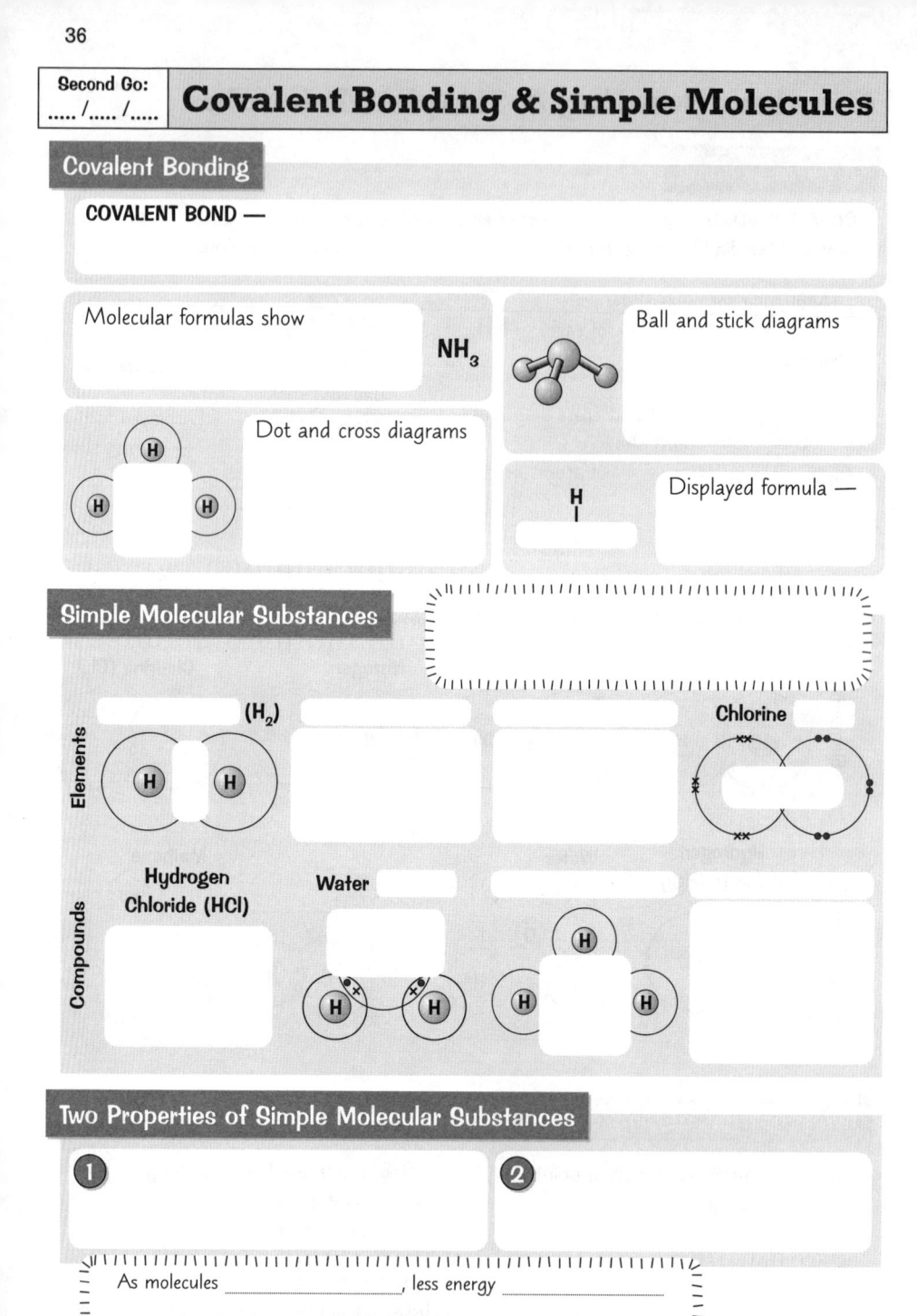

Covalent Bonding & Simple Molecules

Second Go: ...../...../.....

Covalent Bonding

COVALENT BOND —

Molecular formulas show

NH_3

Ball and stick diagrams

Dot and cross diagrams

Displayed formula —

Simple Molecular Substances

Elements

(H_2)

Chlorine

Compounds

Hydrogen Chloride (HCl)

Water

Two Properties of Simple Molecular Substances

1.

2.

As molecules _____, less energy _____.

Topic 2 — Bonding, Structure and Properties of Matter

Covalent Structures

First Go: ..... /..... /.....

Polymers

POLYMERS — very long _____ of _____.

They're usually _____ at room temperature because they have _____.

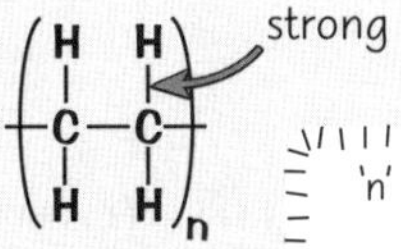

(diagram of polymer with H H / C-C / H H repeating unit, n)

strong _____ bonds
'n' is a large _____

Giant Covalent Structures

GIANT COVALENT STRUCTURES — _____ containing atoms which are _____ by _____ covalent bonds.

High melting and boiling points — _____ to overcome _____ covalent bonds.

Don't conduct _____ (with a couple of exceptions) — no _____ to carry charge.

Examples include: _____, graphite and _____ (silica).

Useful in _____ and composites.

Carbon Allotropes

	Diamond 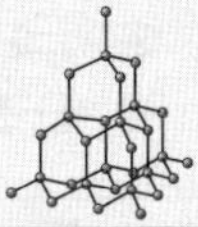	Graphite 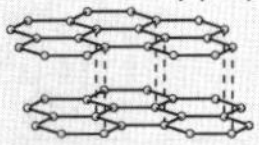	Graphene 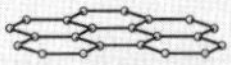
Bonding	C atoms form _____ covalent bonds	C atoms form _____ covalent bonds. No covalent bonds between _____	C atoms form _____ covalent bonds
Properties	Very _____	Soft, _____	_____, light
Melting Point	High		
Conductivity	Doesn't conduct	Conducts electricity and _____ energy	_____ electricity

Each carbon atom in graphite and graphene has _____ electron.

FULLERENES — have _____ shapes. _____ rings of _____ (sometimes 5 or 7)

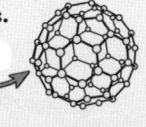

Buckminsterfullerene (_____) is _____ and was the first to be discovered.

NANOTUBES — _____ fullerenes used in nanotechnology, _____ and materials. They have high _____ ratios.

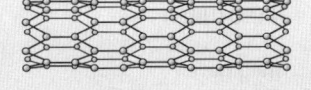

Topic 2 — Bonding, Structure and Properties of Matter

Second Go: ..... / ..... / .....

Covalent Structures

Polymers

POLYMERS —

They're usually

← strong

'n' is

Giant Covalent Structures

GIANT COVALENT STRUCTURES —

High melting and

Don't conduct

Examples include:

Useful in

Carbon Allotropes

	C atoms form	C atoms form	C atoms form
Bonding			
Properties			
Melting Point			
Conductivity			

Each carbon atom in

FULLERENES —

rings of

Buckminsterfullerene
and was the first to be discovered.

NANOTUBES —

They have

Topic 2 — Bonding, Structure and Properties of Matter

Mixed Practice Quizzes

You're halfway through Topic 2, so it's about time you did some quizzes to see how much you've picked up from p.33-38. Mark your answers when you're finished.

Quiz 1 — Date: ...... / ...... / ......

1) What is the charge on an ion of a Group 6 element?
2) Give one property of substances with giant covalent structures.
3) Which type of bonding occurs between a metal and a non-metal?
4) Why do ionic compounds have high melting and boiling points?
5) How many bonds do carbon atoms form in a diamond structure?
6) What do the shapes of fullerenes have in common?
7) Why can simple molecular substances not conduct electricity?
8) Describe the dot and cross structure of a hydrogen molecule.
9) Why can graphite and graphene conduct electricity?
10) What type of attraction is involved in ionic bonding?

Total:

Quiz 2 — Date: ...... / ...... / ......

1) What type of ion do Group 1 elements form?
2) What is meant by ionic bonding?
3) Name a carbon allotrope which is a thermal conductor.
4) In simple molecular substances, which are stronger — the covalent bonds or the forces between molecules?
5) How many covalent bonds are there in a water molecule?
6) Give one limitation of dot and cross diagrams.
7) Describe what a polymer is.
8) Do metals lose electrons or gain electrons in order to form ions?
9) What name is given to cylindrical fullerenes?
10) Give one example of a simple molecular substance.

Total:

Mixed Practice Quizzes

Quiz 3 Date: ...... / ...... / ......

1) What are the properties of graphene?
2) Give three examples of giant covalent substances.
3) Give one limitation of a ball and stick diagram.
4) What states are simple molecular substances usually in at room temperature?
5) Which allotrope is a single layer of covalently bonded carbon atoms?
6) What can be described as 'a very long chain of repeating units'?
7) Which carbon allotrope's structure can contain rings of five, six or seven carbon atoms?
8) Why are polymers usually solid at room temperature?
9) What type of structure do ionic compounds have?
10) What name is given to a shared pair of electrons between two non-metal atoms?

Total:

Quiz 4 Date: ...... / ...... / ......

1) Name one carbon allotrope that does not conduct electricity.
2) How many electrons are shared between the two atoms in a nitrogen molecule?
3) Do non-metals form positive ions or negative ions?
4) True or false? Nanotubes have low length to diameter ratios.
5) How many electrons does sodium lose to form a sodium ion?
6) In which states will ionic compounds conduct electricity?
7) What type of bonding occurs in sodium chloride?
8) Name the fullerene with the molecular formula C_{60}.
9) Which type of diagram should you use if you want to show the 3D structure of a molecule?
10) True or false? Smaller molecules require more energy to break the forces between them than larger molecules.

Total:

Metallic Bonding

First Go:
...../...../.....

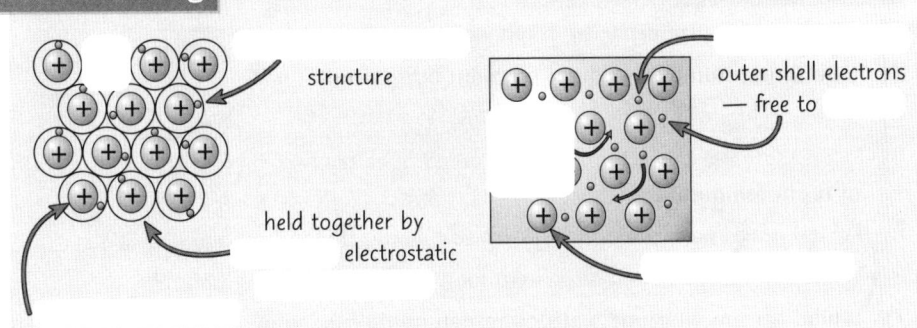

Metallic Bonding

_____ structure

held together by electrostatic _____

outer shell electrons — free to _____

Four Properties of Metals

1. High melting and boiling points — lots of _____ needed to overcome _____.

2. Good thermal conductors — energy _____ by _____ electrons.

3. Good electrical conductors — _____.

4. Soft and malleable — layers in metals _____.

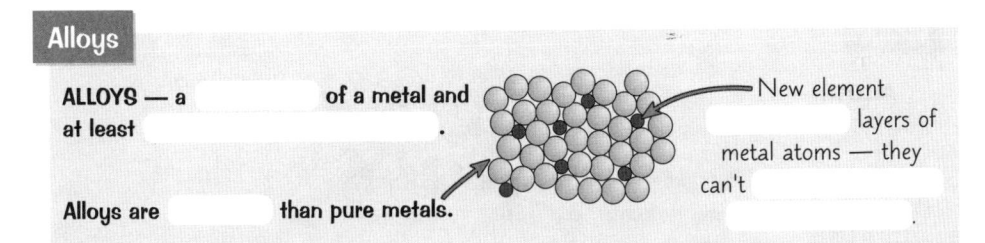

Alloys

ALLOYS — a _____ of a metal and at least _____.

Alloys are _____ than pure metals.

New element _____ layers of metal atoms — they can't _____.

Topic 2 — Bonding, Structure and Properties of Matter

Metallic Bonding

Second Go: ..... / ..... / .....

Metallic Bonding

outer shell electrons

held together by

Four Properties of Metals

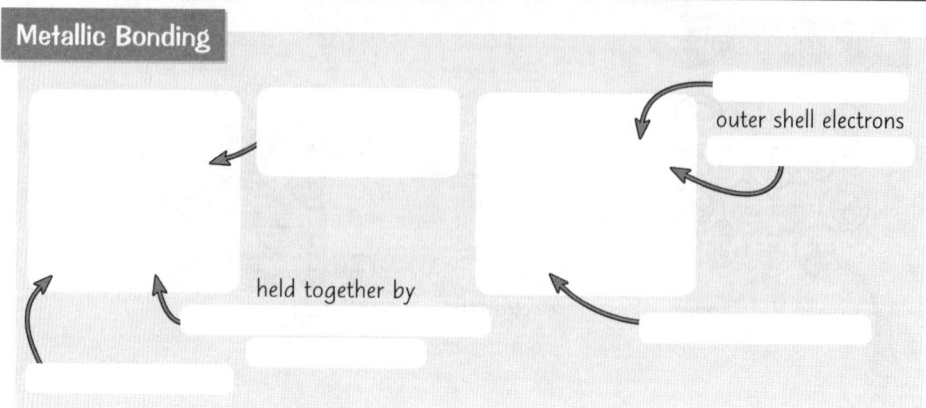

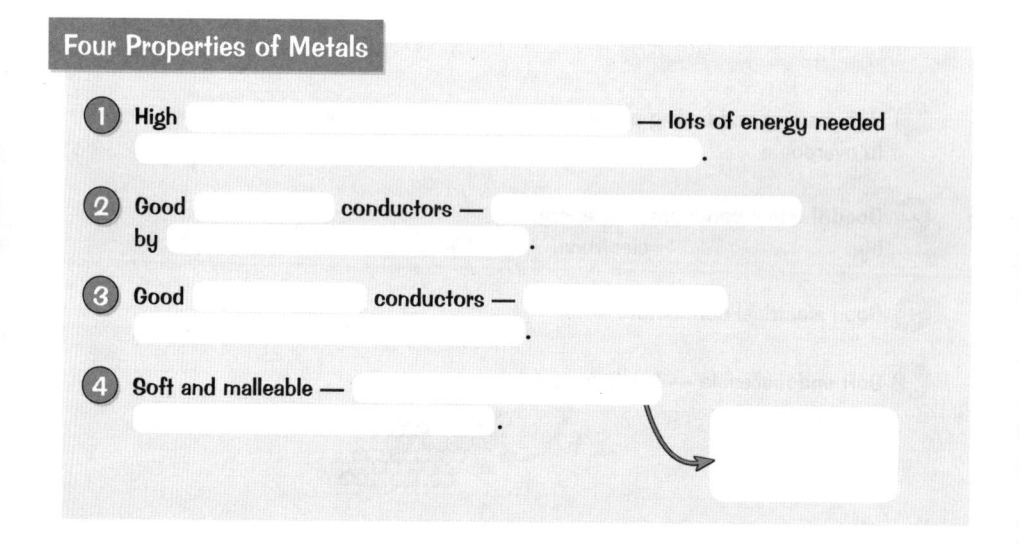

1. High _____ — lots of energy needed _____.

2. Good _____ conductors — _____ by _____.

3. Good _____ conductors — _____.

4. Soft and malleable — _____.

Alloys

ALLOYS — _____

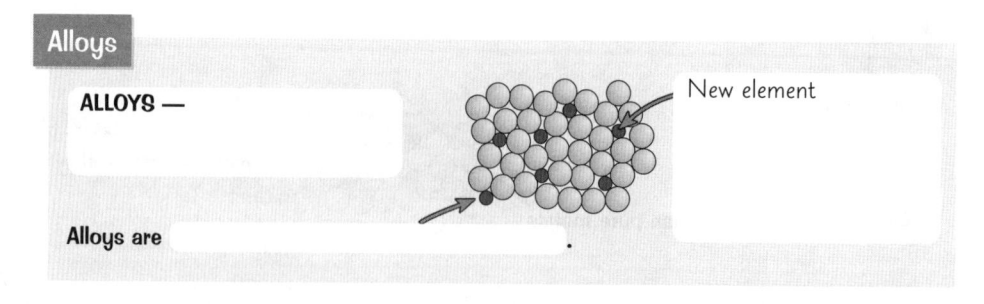

New element

Alloys are _____.

Topic 2 — Bonding, Structure and Properties of Matter

States of Matter and Changing State

First Go: ..... /..... /.....

Particle Theory

	Solid		Gas
Particle Diagram	(diagram)		(diagram)
Particle Arrangement			Random
Particle Movement	Fixed position, vibrate		Move in all
Particle Closeness	close together		

Particle theory doesn't show the particles. Particles aren't .... between spheres.

Atoms don't have the .... properties of ....

Changes of State

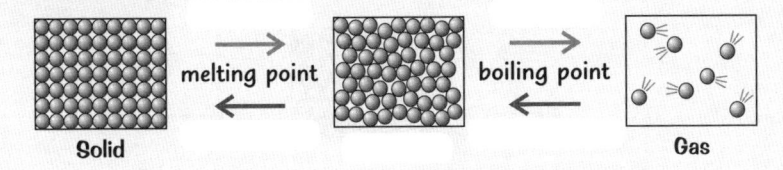

Solid → melting point → (liquid) → boiling point → Gas
(and reverse arrows)

Melting and Boiling:
heats up → Particles gain .... → Forces between particles .... → .... break free from ....

Condensing and Freezing:
cools down → Particles lose .... → Forces between particles .... → .... held in ....

The .... to change state is linked to the strength of .... Stronger .... melting and boiling point.

State Symbols

	(l)		(aq)
solid			

Topic 2 — Bonding, Structure and Properties of Matter

States of Matter and Changing State

Second Go: ...../...../.....

Particle Theory

Particle Diagram			
Particle Arrangement			
Particle Movement			
Particle Closeness			

Particle theory

Particles

Atoms don't ....

Changes of State

Melting and .... :

Substance → Particles → Forces → Particles

.... and Freezing:

Substance → Particles → Forces → Particles

The amount of energy needed

State Symbols

Topic 2 — Bonding, Structure and Properties of Matter

Nanoparticles and their Uses

First Go: ..... /..... /.....

Particle Sizes

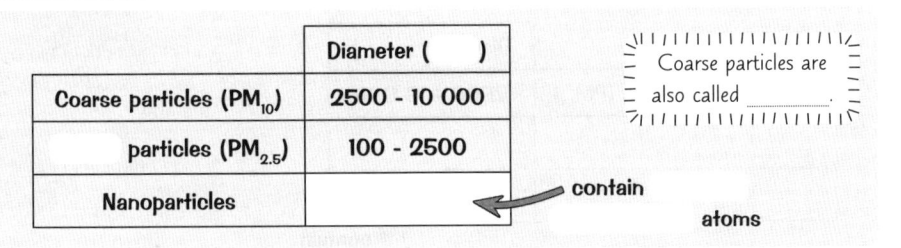

	Diameter ( )
Coarse particles (PM$_{10}$)	2500 - 10 000
.... particles (PM$_{2.5}$)	100 - 2500
Nanoparticles	

Coarse particles are also called ....

← contain .... atoms

surface area to volume ratio = ...

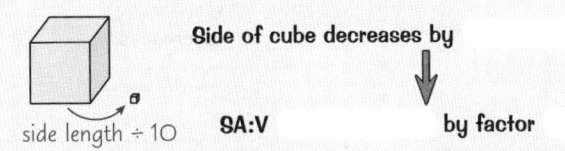

side length ÷ 10   Side of cube decreases by ....

SA:V .... by factor ....

The .... surface area to volume ratio of nanoparticles means .... may be different to those of ....

Uses of Nanoparticles

....

....

sun cream

deodorant

....

....

Finding .... nanoparticles is .... scientific research.

Evaluating Uses

Advantages

Generally more .... than .... without nanoparticles.

.... may be needed compared to materials with '............' particles.

Disadvantages

Long-term effects on .... aren't ....

Could .... to the environment if ....

Topic 2 — Bonding, Structure and Properties of Matter

Second Go:
...../...../.....

Nanoparticles and their Uses

Particle Sizes

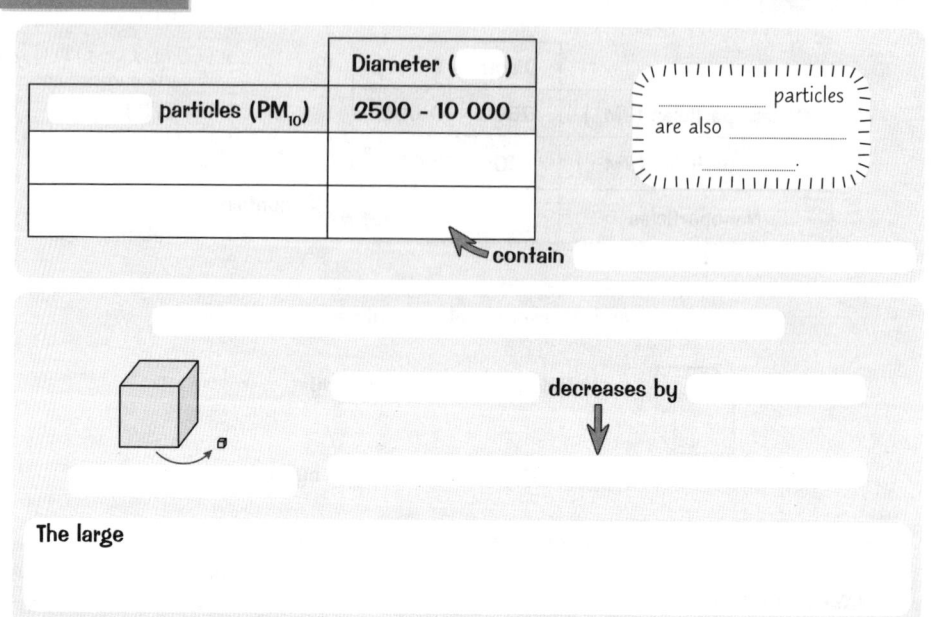

	Diameter ( )
.... particles (PM$_{10}$)	2500 - 10 000

↖ contain

.... particles are also ....

[diagram of cube with side a]

....

decreases by ↓

....

The large ....

Uses of Nanoparticles

....

....

....

....

....

....

Finding

Evaluating Uses

Advantages
Generally
Smaller

Disadvantages
Long-term
Could cause

Topic 2 — Bonding, Structure and Properties of Matter

Mixed Practice Quizzes

Hope you've got your head round all those state changes, because it's quiz time. These four will test you on the information covered on p.41-46. Let's get to it.

Quiz 1   Date: ...... / ...... / ......

1) True or false? Nanoparticles have a small surface area to volume ratio.
2) Give two properties of metals.
3) Which state of matter contains a regular arrangement of particles?
4) What is meant by the term 'alloy'?
5) Do individual atoms have the bulk properties of materials made from them?
6) Describe the movement of particles in a gas.
7) What name is given to particles with a diameter between 100 nm and 2500 nm?
8) What is the state symbol for a liquid?
9) Why do metals have high boiling points?
10) What is the typical diameter of a nanoparticle?

Total:

Quiz 2   Date: ...... / ...... / ......

1) What happens to the outer shell electrons in metallic bonding?
2) What happens to the layers of atoms in a metal when a new element is added to form an alloy?
3) Describe the arrangement of particles in a liquid.
4) Which states of matter does a substance change between when it boils?
5) What are two limitations of particle theory?
6) How do you calculate surface area to volume ratio?
7) True or false? The particles gain energy when a substance freezes.
8) What name is given to the transition from liquid to solid?
9) Give two examples of common uses of nanoparticles.
10) What is the state symbol for a gas?

Total:

Topic 2 — Bonding, Structure and Properties of Matter

Mixed Practice Quizzes

Quiz 3   Date: ...... / ...... / ......

1) How close together are the particles in a gas?
2) How does the strength of the forces between particles affect the melting and boiling points of a substance?
3) Why are alloys harder than pure metals?
4) Explain why metals are good thermal conductors.
5) Which two changes of state involve a substance losing energy?
6) What does the state symbol (aq) tell you about a substance?
7) Give two disadvantages of nanoparticles.
8) Which state of matter contains vibrating particles that are fixed in position?
9) What happens to the particles when a substance melts?
10) True or false? Surface area to volume ratio can affect a material's properties.

Total:

Quiz 4   Date: ...... / ...... / ......

1) When a substance condenses, do the particles gain energy or lose energy?
2) Which state of matter is indicated by the symbol (s)?
3) True or false? Metals melt at very low temperatures.
4) What type of attraction holds a metallic structure together?
5) Why are metals malleable?
6) What process occurs when a substance goes from a solid to a liquid?
7) If the side length of a cube decreases by a factor of 10, what happens to the surface area to volume ratio?
8) What type of substance is produced when metal atoms are mixed with the atoms of another element?
9) Which state of matter consists of particles that are close together but are moving round each other?
10) Give one advantage of using nanoparticles.

Total:

Topic 3 — Quantitative Chemistry

Mass and the Mole

First Go: ..../..../....

Relative Formula Mass

RELATIVE FORMULA MASS ( ) — sum of _____ of the atoms in the _____.

Percentage mass of _____ = $\dfrac{\rule{3cm}{0.4pt}}{\rule{3cm}{0.4pt}} \times$

Balanced Equations

BALANCED EQUATION — equation with _____ of atoms of each element on _____.

....Mg + O$_2$ → ....MgO

In a _____:

Sum of the _____ of the _____ = Sum of the _____ of the _____

The Mole

One mole = 6.02×10^{23} _____ of a substance. ← This is the _____

The _____ could be e.g. _____, _____, ions or electrons.

Mass in _____ of an element = the _____ mole of atoms of the element.

Mass in _____ of a compound = the _____ mole of molecules of the compound.

Number of moles ( ) =

Conservation of Mass

No atoms are _____ in a _____ reaction, so the total masses of reactants and products are also _____ — MASS IS _____.

If you weigh an _____ reaction vessel, sometimes you'll see a _____:

DECREASE in mass — a gas _____ during the reaction and _____ the _____ vessel, so its mass is _____.

INCREASE in mass — a gas _____ , so its mass _____ is _____ the mass in the vessel (none of the _____ are gaseous).

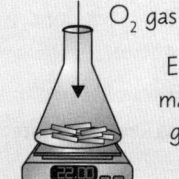

CO$_2$ gas _____

E.g. the _____ of calcium carbonate produces CO$_2$ gas.

O$_2$ gas _____

E.g. the reaction of magnesium with O$_2$ gas only produces _____.

Topic 3 — Quantitative Chemistry

Mass and the Mole

Second Go: ..... / ..... / .....

Relative Formula Mass

RELATIVE FORMULA MASS (   ) — _____ .

Percentage mass of _____ = _____

Balanced Equations

BALANCED EQUATION — _____

_____ Mg + O_2 → ....

In a _____ :

_____ = _____

The Mole

One mole = _____ of a substance.

Mass in _____

Mass in _____

Number of moles (   ) = _____

Conservation of Mass

No atoms _____

If you _____

DECREASE in mass — _____

INCREASE in mass — _____

E.g. the _____ of calcium carbonate produces _____ gas.

E.g. the reaction of magnesium with _____ gas only _____ .

Topic 3 — Quantitative Chemistry

Moles, Equations & Limiting Reactants

First Go: ..... /..... /.....

Moles and Equations

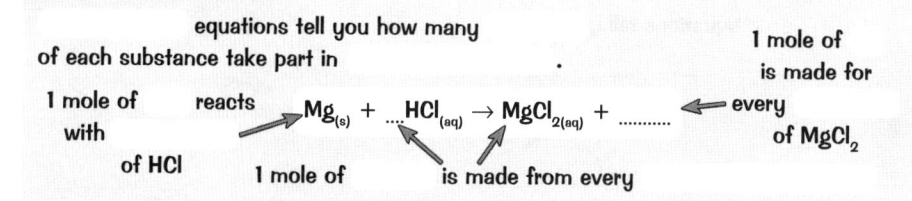

equations tell you how many of each substance take part in .

1 mole of .... reacts with .... of HCl

1 mole of .... is made from every ....

$Mg_{(s)} + ...HCl_{(aq)} \rightarrow MgCl_{2(aq)} + ...$

1 mole of .... is made for every .... of $MgCl_2$

Balancing Equations Using Masses

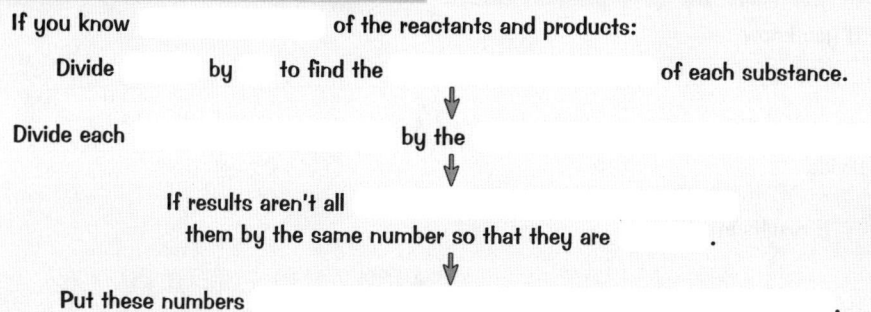

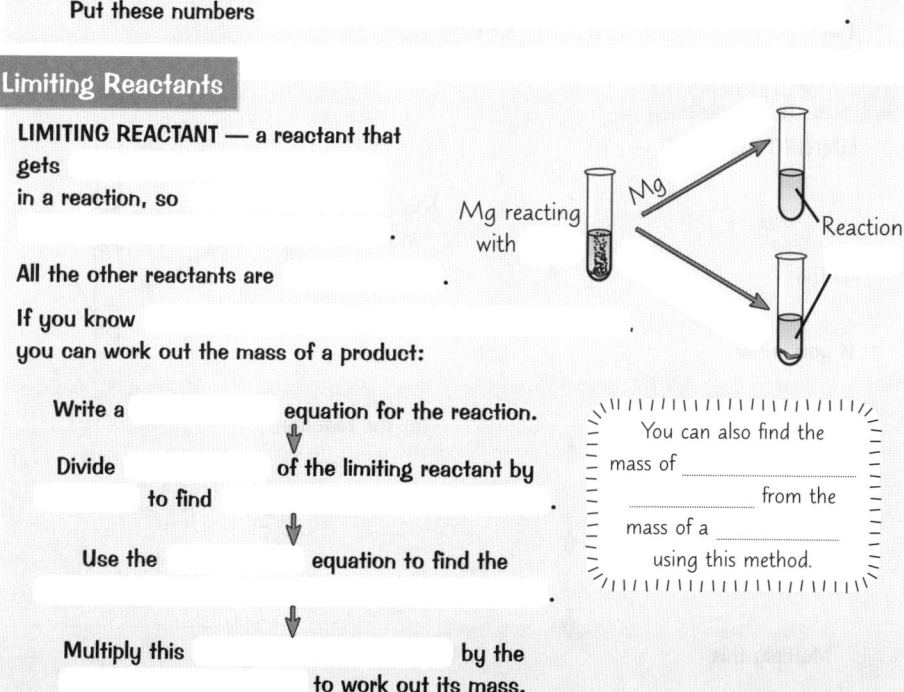

If you know .... of the reactants and products:

Divide .... by .... to find the .... of each substance.

Divide each .... by the ....

If results aren't all .... them by the same number so that they are ....

Put these numbers ....

Limiting Reactants

LIMITING REACTANT — a reactant that gets .... in a reaction, so ....

All the other reactants are ....

If you know .... you can work out the mass of a product:

Write a .... equation for the reaction.

Divide .... of the limiting reactant by .... to find ....

Use the .... equation to find the ....

Multiply this .... by the .... to work out its mass.

Mg reacting with ....   Reaction ....

You can also find the mass of .... from the mass of a .... using this method.

Topic 3 — Quantitative Chemistry

Second Go: ..... /..... /.....
Moles, Equations & Limiting Reactants

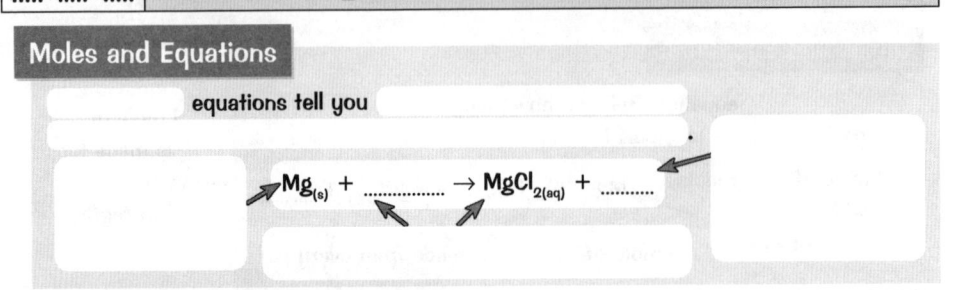

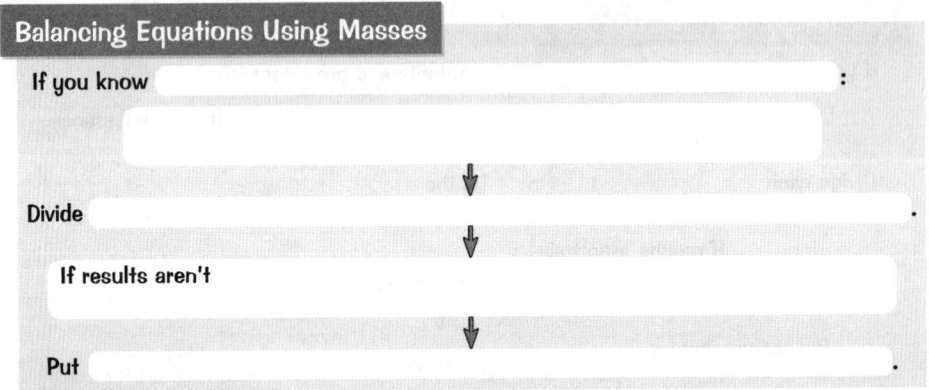

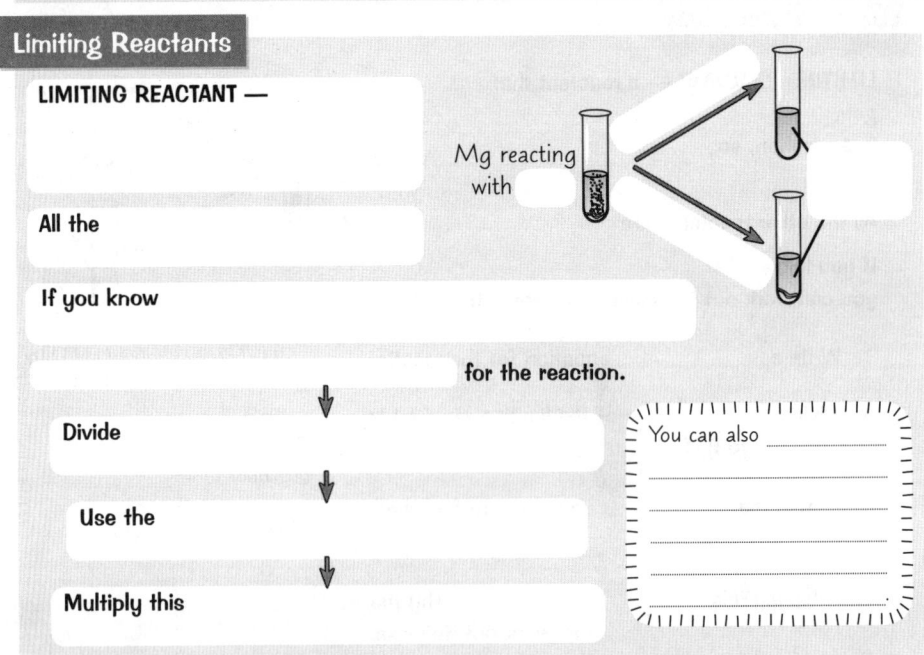

Moles and Equations

.... equations tell you ....

$Mg_{(s)}$ + ... → $MgCl_{2(aq)}$ + ...

Balancing Equations Using Masses

If you know .... :

Divide ....

If results aren't ....

Put ....

Limiting Reactants

LIMITING REACTANT — ....

Mg reacting with ....

All the ....

If you know ....

.... for the reaction.

Divide ....

Use the ....

Multiply this ....

You can also ....

Topic 3 — Quantitative Chemistry

Gases and Concentrations

First Go: ...../...../......

Gases

At .... temperature and pressure, one .... will occupy ....

At room temperature and pressure, one .... occupies 24 ....

At r.t.p.:

Volume of .... = $\dfrac{\text{Mass}}{M_r}$ × ....

Room temperature and pressure (r.t.p.) = ... °C and .... atm

Concentration

CONCENTRATION — amount of .... dissolved in a certain ....

Increase the...	Concentration...
...amount of	
...volume of	

Two ways to measure concentration:

Concentration = ...	Units
.... of solute / .... of solvent	/dm³
.... of solute / .... of solvent	/dm³

You can .... between these units by using the .... equation.

Calculating Concentration from Titrations

Titrations let you find the .... of one solution needed to .... with ....

To find an unknown concentration from .... :

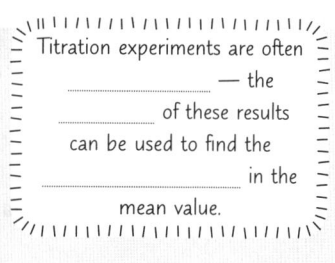

Reactant 1: .... volume, ... concentration

Reactant 2: .... volume, ... concentration (+ indicator)

Titration experiments are often .... — the .... of these results can be used to find the .... in the mean value.

Multiply .... by .... to work out .... of reactant 1.

↓

Use .... to work out how many .... have reacted.

↓

Divide .... of reactant 2 by .... to get the .... concentration.

Topic 3 — Quantitative Chemistry

Gases and Concentrations

Second Go: ...../...../.....

Gases

At the same

At room

At   :

☐ = ☐

Room temperature and pressure (_____) =

Concentration

CONCENTRATION —

Increase the...	Concentration...

Two ways to measure concentration:

Concentration = ...	Units

You can _____ by using the _____.

Titration experiments are _____
_____
_____
_____
_____.

Calculating Concentration from Titrations

Titrations

To find an unknown concentration from _____:

Reactant 1:

Reactant 2:

Multiply

⬇

Use reaction

⬇

Divide

Topic 3 — Quantitative Chemistry

Atom Economy and Percentage Yield

First Go: ..... / ..... / .....

Atom Economy

ATOM ECONOMY (_____) — _____ of the mass of reactants that ends up as _____ .

$$\text{Atom economy} = \frac{}{} \times 100$$

Three advantages of using reactions with _____ atom economies:

① Use up _____ at a _____ rate.

② _____ a lot of waste.

③ _____

→ This means they are _____ .

When choosing a reaction pathway, the _____ , rate, _____ , atom economy and usefulness of _____ are all considered.

Percentage Yield

YIELD — the _____ made in a reaction.
_____ — _____ of the amount of product you actually get (_____) with the maximum _____ .

$$\text{Percentage yield} = \frac{}{} \times 100$$

_____ % yield = _____ waste + _____ costs

Factors Affecting the Yield

Yields are always _____ than _____ %.

Three common reasons for this:

① Reaction is not _____ — e.g. it's _____ .

② _____ use up some of the reactants or product.

③ Some product is _____ from the reaction mixture.

Second Go: ..... / ..... / .....

Atom Economy and Percentage Yield

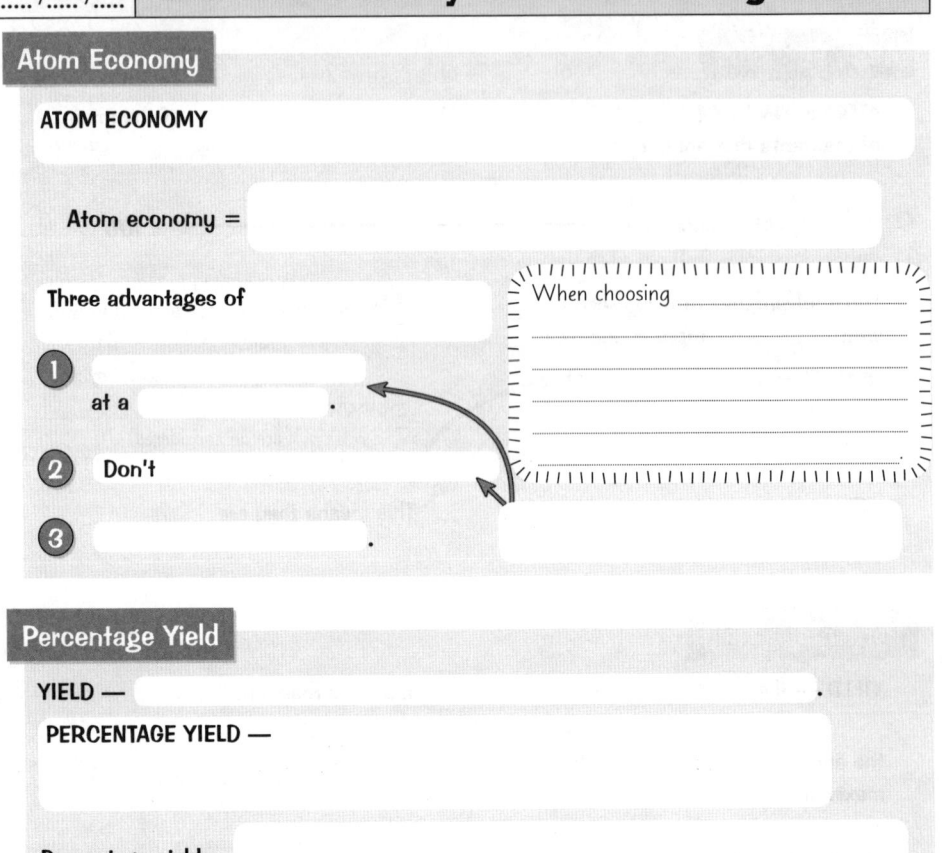

Atom Economy

ATOM ECONOMY

Atom economy =

Three advantages of

1. _____ at a _____ .

2. Don't

3. _____ .

When choosing _____

Percentage Yield

YIELD — _____ .

PERCENTAGE YIELD —

Percentage yield =

_____ % yield = _____

Factors Affecting the Yield

Yields are always _____ .

Three _____ for this:

1. _____ — e.g. it's _____ .

2. _____ .

3. Some _____ from the reaction mixture.

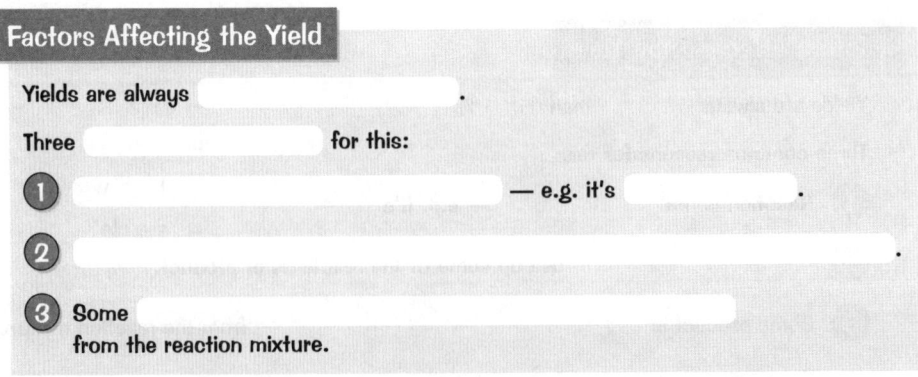

Topic 3 — Quantitative Chemistry

Mixed Practice Quizzes

It's time for a few (well forty to be precise) questions to test what you've covered on p.49-56. Mark each test yourself to check how brilliantly you've done.

Quiz 1   Date: ...... / ...... / ......

1) Give a definition of the term 'concentration'.
2) What name is given to the reactant that's completely used up in a reaction?
3) What is the definition of 'relative formula mass'?
4) Why might the mass of a reaction vessel decrease during a reaction?
5) Give one reason why a reaction percentage yield may be lower than 100%.
6) What is meant by the term 'balanced equation'?
7) What volume is occupied by one mole of gas at r.t.p.?
8) Explain how to use the results of a titration to find an unknown concentration of a solution.
9) Give two advantages of using reactions with higher atom economies.
10) Give the equation for calculating percentage yield.

Total:

Quiz 2   Date: ...... / ...... / ......

1) How many particles are in one mole of a substance?
2) What happens to a reaction when the limiting reactant has been completely used up?
3) What is the difference between 'yield' and 'percentage yield'?
4) How could you use the limiting reactant mass to find the product mass?
5) Give two units of concentration.
6) How does increasing the amount of solute affect the concentration of a solution?
7) True or false? Atoms can be destroyed in a chemical reaction.
8) True or false? Reactions with high atom economies produce lots of waste.
9) How is the yield of a reaction affected when the reaction is reversible?
10) Suggest why the mass of a reaction vessel might increase during a reaction.

Total:

Topic 3 — Quantitative Chemistry

Mixed Practice Quizzes

Quiz 3 Date: ...... / ...... / ......

1) What is equal to the mass in grams of one mole of atoms of an element?
2) Give a definition of the term 'atom economy'.
3) How do the total masses of reactants and products in a reaction compare?
4) What do the large numbers in front of chemical formulas in a balanced equation represent?
5) True or false? r.t.p. = 20 °C and 1 atm.
6) How can you use mass and M_r to find the number of moles of a substance?
7) Give the equation used to find the volume of a gas at r.t.p.
8) Which equation can be used to convert between mol/dm^3 and g/dm^3?
9) Are reactions with higher atom economies more or less sustainable?
10) What term is given to the sum of the relative atomic masses in a formula?

Total:

Quiz 4 Date: ...... / ...... / ......

1) How could you describe the reactants in a reaction that aren't limiting?
2) How would a reduction in percentage yield affect the cost of a reaction?
3) Give an equation that could be used to work out the percentage mass of an element in a compound.
4) How would the mass of a reaction vessel change if a gaseous reactant from the air takes part in the reaction?
5) How many moles of $MgCl_2$ are produced if one mole of Mg is reacted with 2 moles of HCl?
6) Which term is given to the amount of substance dissolved in a certain volume of solution?
7) How does increasing solvent volume affect the concentration of a solution?
8) True or false? One mole of a substance contains 6.03×10^{22} particles.
9) Give an equation used to calculate the atom economy of a reaction.
10) True or false? At the same temperature and pressure, one mole of any gas will occupy the same volume.

Total:

Topic 3 — Quantitative Chemistry

Topic 4 — Chemical Changes

Acids, Bases and their Reactions

First Go: ..... / ..... / .....

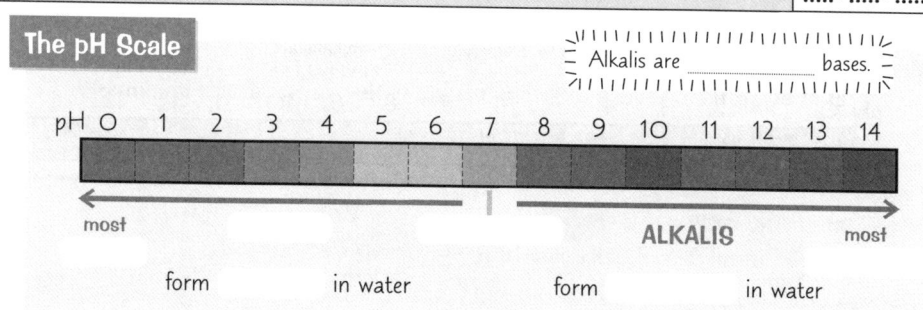

The pH Scale

Alkalis are .... bases.

pH 0 1 2 3 4 5 6 7 8 9 10 11 12 13 14

most .... ALKALIS most

.... form .... in water   .... form .... in water

Two Ways to Measure pH

1 UNIVERSAL INDICATOR —
a wide range ....

depending on ....
It gives ....
pH value.

2 pH PROBE —
gives ....
.... of the pH.

Neutralisation Reactions

.... + base $\rightarrow$ salt + ...

The products of neutralisation reactions are ....

.... + $OH^-_{(aq)}$ $\rightarrow$ ....

Titrations

TITRATIONS (using a suitable ....)
— used to find the ....
.... of acid needed to
.... of alkali (or vice versa).
The results can be used to calculate the
....

Reactions of Acids

To get the formula of a salt, ... the charges of the ions so the .... is ....

acid + ... $\rightarrow$ salt + ... + carbon dioxide

acid + metal oxide $\rightarrow$ .... + ...

acid + metal hydroxide $\rightarrow$ .... + ...

Soluble salts are made by adding ....
or ....
to .... The excess .... is filtered
off and the remaining salt solution
is ....

Acid Used	Salt Produced
HCl	
H_2SO_4	
HNO_3	

The first part of a salt's name comes from .... in the base, alkali or carbonate.

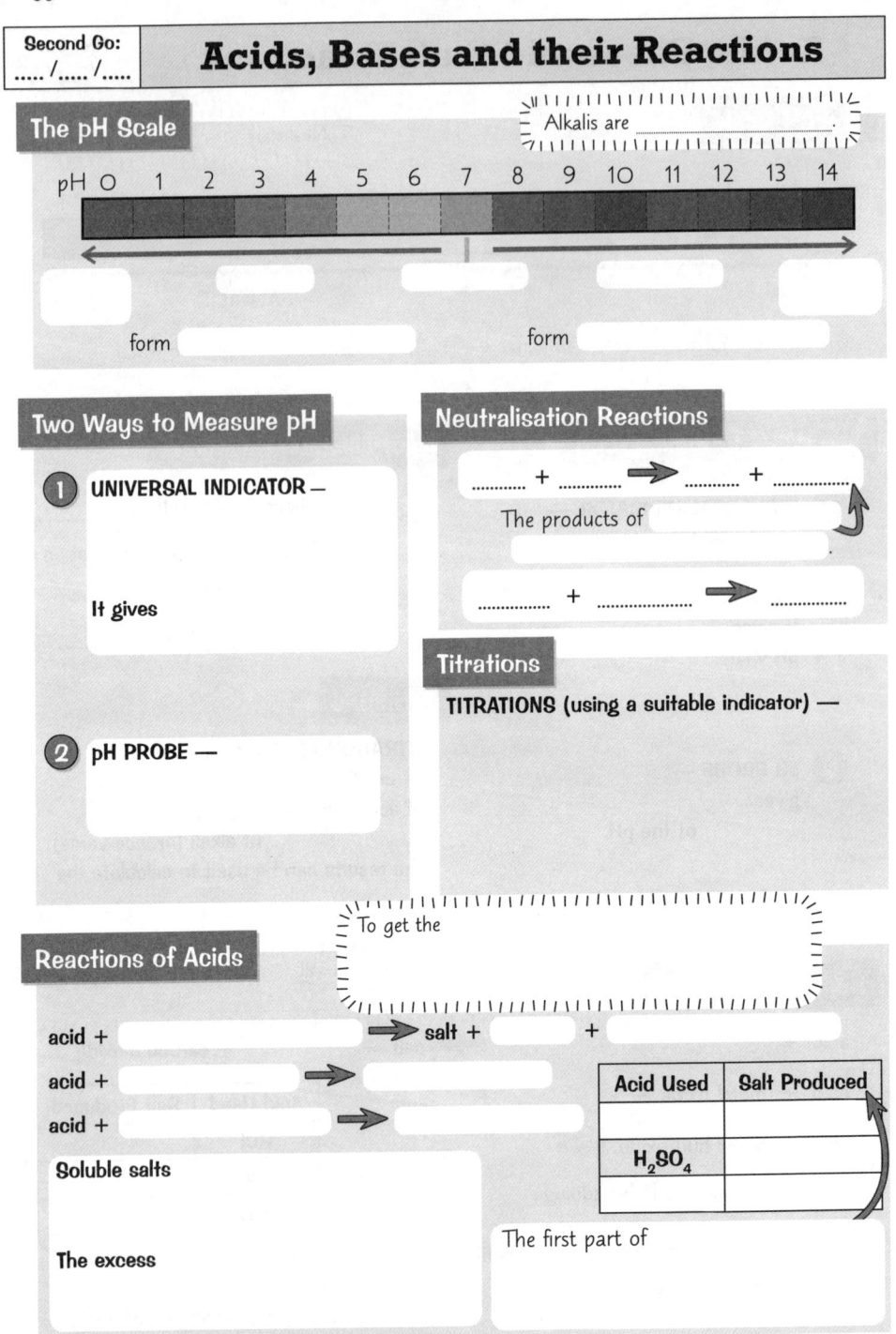

Second Go: ..../..../....

Acids, Bases and their Reactions

The pH Scale

Alkalis are _____.

pH 0 1 2 3 4 5 6 7 8 9 10 11 12 13 14

_____   _____   _____   _____

form _____   form _____

Two Ways to Measure pH

① UNIVERSAL INDICATOR —

It gives

② pH PROBE —

Neutralisation Reactions

...... + ... → ...... + ...

The products of _____

...... + ... → ......

Titrations

TITRATIONS (using a suitable indicator) —

Reactions of Acids

To get the _____

acid + _____ → salt + _____ + _____

acid + _____ → _____

acid + _____ → _____

Soluble salts

The excess

Acid Used	Salt Produced
H_2SO_4	

The first part of

Topic 4 — Chemical Changes

Strong and Weak Acids

First Go: ...../...../.....

Acid Strength

	Definition	Examples
_____ acid	An acid that _____ ionises (_____) in water to produce _____ ions.	hydrochloric acid _____ acid _____ acid
WEAK acid	An acid that _____ in water to produce _____ ions.	_____ acid citric acid _____ acid

pH and H⁺ Ion Concentration

pH — a measure of the _____ in a solution.

When the pH of a _____ changes by X...

...the _____ changes by a factor of _____ .

For a given concentration of acid, as the acid strength _____ , pH _____ .

The pH of a strong acid is always _____ the pH of a weaker acid at _____ .

Strength vs Concentration

	A measure of...
ACID STRENGTH	...the proportion of _____ that _____ in water.
ACID CONCENTRATION	...the number of _____ in _____ of water.

Dilute acids have a _____ concentration.

The pH will _____ with increasing acid _____ regardless of whether _____ .

Topic 4 — Chemical Changes

Second Go: ...../...../.....

Strong and Weak Acids

Acid Strength

STRONG acid	Definition:	Examples:
WEAK acid	Definition:	Examples:

pH and H^+ Ion Concentration

pH — .

When the pH

For a given

The pH of .... the pH of .... at ....

Strength vs Concentration

ACID STRENGTH	A measure of...
ACID CONCENTRATION	A measure of...

Dilute acids have ....

The pH

Topic 4 — Chemical Changes

Reactivity of Metals

First Go: ...../...../.....

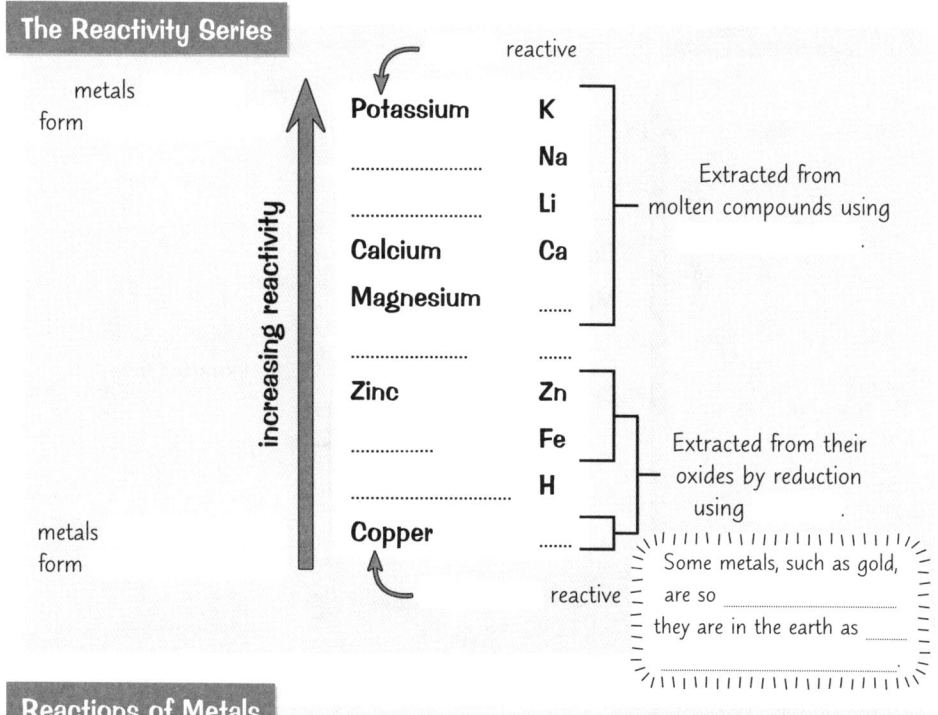

The Reactivity Series

metals form

increasing reactivity

reactive

- Potassium — K
- .... — Na
- .... — Li
- Calcium — Ca
- Magnesium — ......

Extracted from molten compounds using ....

- .... —
- Zinc — Zn
- .... — Fe
- .... — H
- Copper — ......

Extracted from their oxides by reduction using ....

metals form

reactive

Some metals, such as gold, are so .... they are in the earth as ....

Reactions of Metals

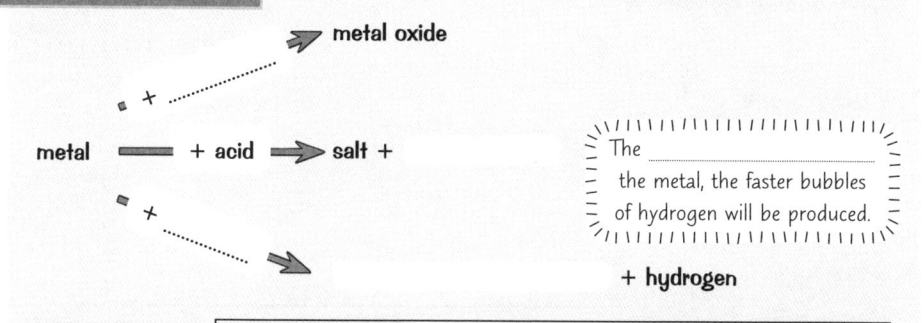

metal + ... → metal oxide

metal + acid → salt + hydrogen

metal + ... → .... + hydrogen

The .... the metal, the faster bubbles of hydrogen will be produced.

reaction with...	K	Na	Li	Ca	Mg	Zn	Fe	Cu
cold, dilute acid			reaction				reaction	no reaction
water								

reactivity →

DISPLACEMENT REACTION — when a more reactive .... a less reactive .... from its compound.

Topic 4 — Chemical Changes

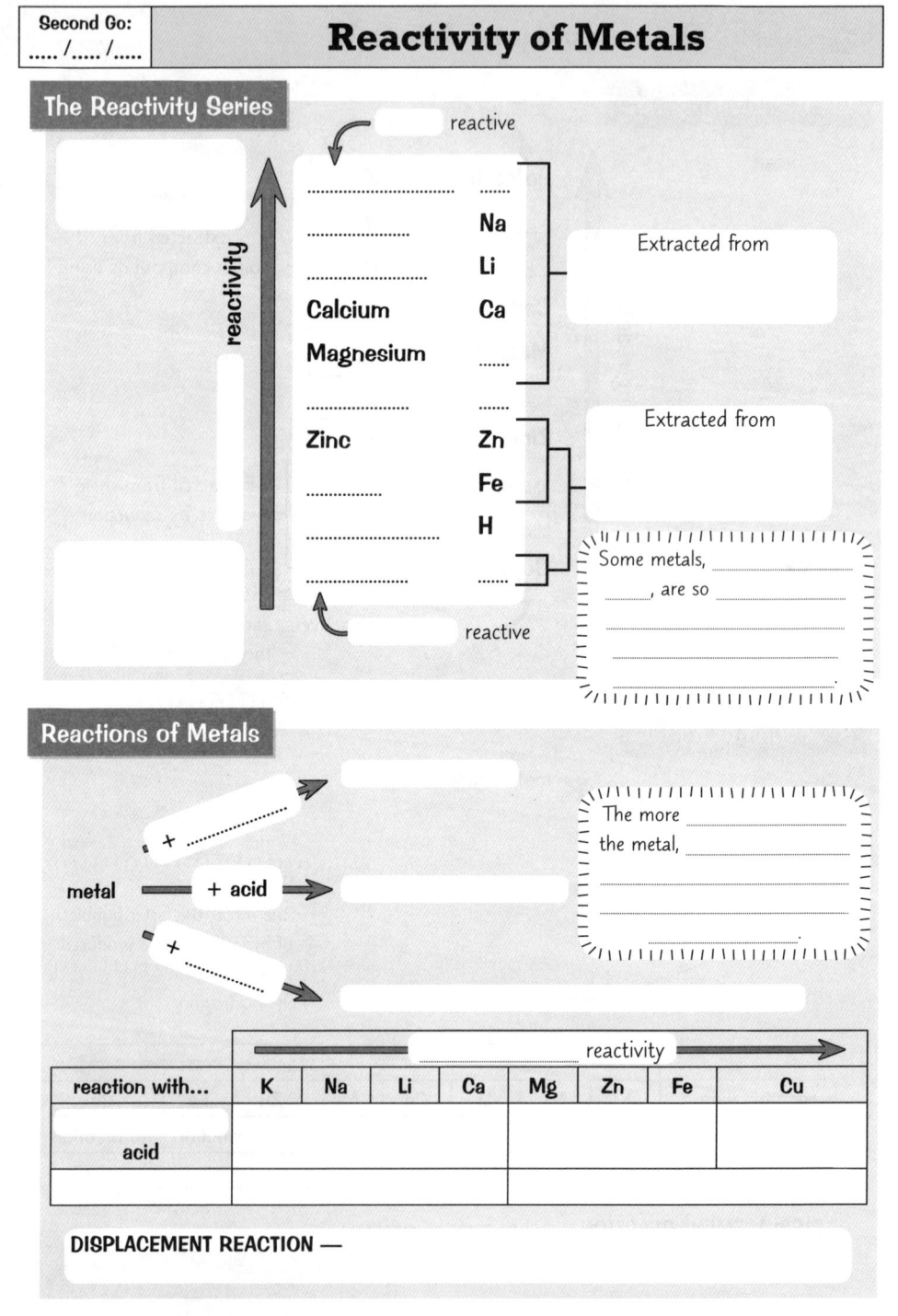

Second Go: ...../...../.....

Reactivity of Metals

The Reactivity Series

.... reactive

....
....
....
Calcium
Magnesium
....
Zinc
....
....
....

Na
Li
Ca
....
....
Zn
Fe
H
....

reactivity ↑

Extracted from ....

Extracted from ....

Some metals, ..., are so ....

.... reactive

Reactions of Metals

metal + acid →

+ .... →
+ acid →
+ .... →

The more .... the metal, ...

reaction with...	← reactivity →							
	K	Na	Li	Ca	Mg	Zn	Fe	Cu
acid								

DISPLACEMENT REACTION — ....

Topic 4 — Chemical Changes

Redox Reactions and Ionic Equations

First Go: ...../...../.....

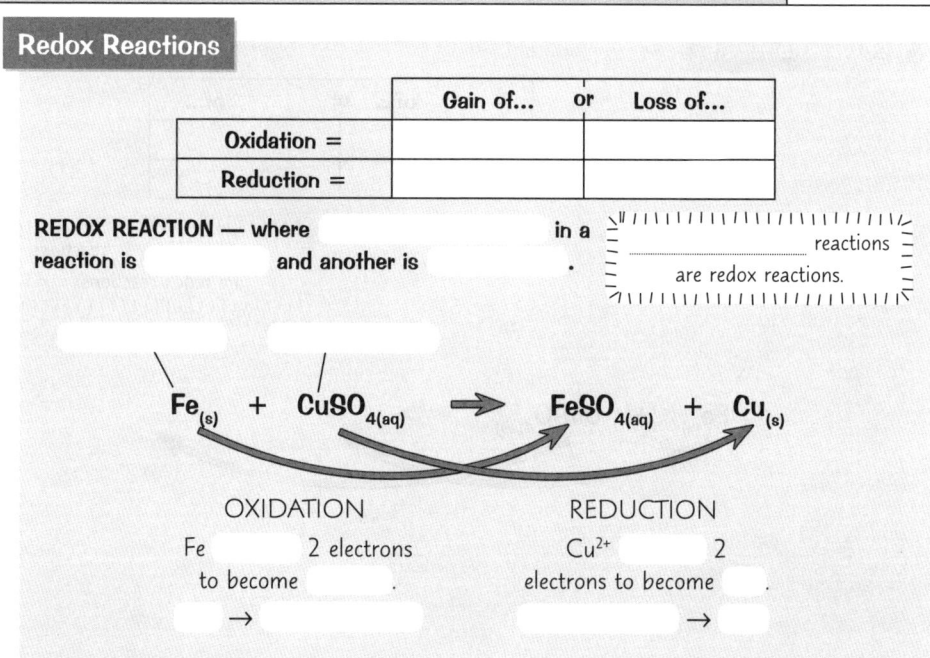

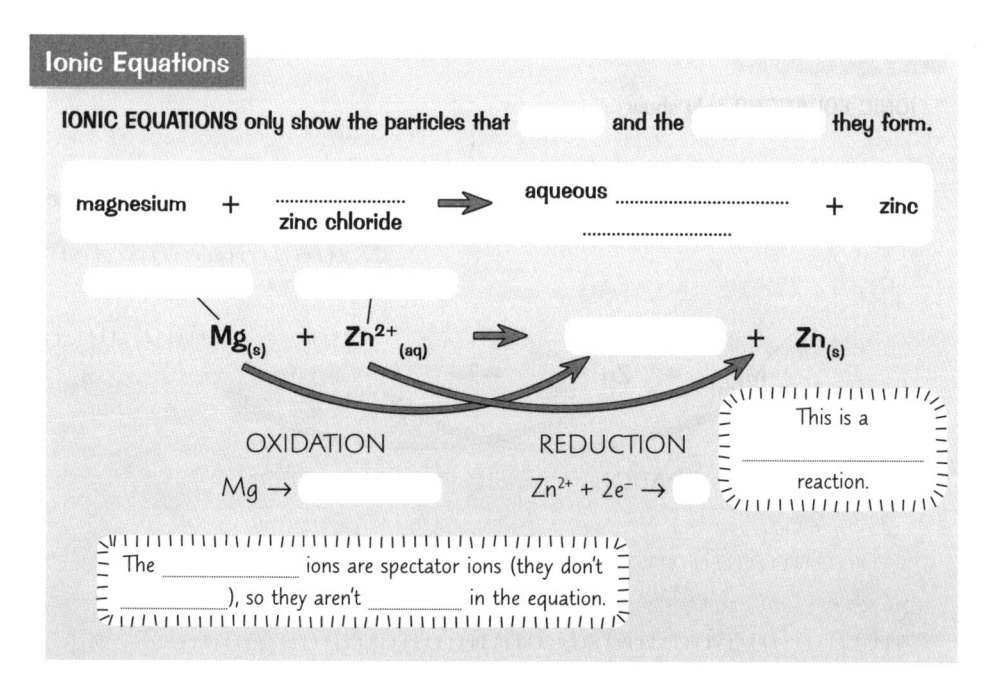

Redox Reactions

	Gain of...	or	Loss of...
Oxidation =			
Reduction =			

REDOX REACTION — where .... in a reaction is .... and another is ....

.... reactions are redox reactions.

$Fe_{(s)} + CuSO_{4(aq)} \rightarrow FeSO_{4(aq)} + Cu_{(s)}$

OXIDATION
Fe .... 2 electrons to become ....
.... → ....

REDUCTION
Cu^{2+} .... 2 electrons to become ....
.... → ....

Ionic Equations

IONIC EQUATIONS only show the particles that .... and the .... they form.

magnesium + zinc chloride → aqueous .... + zinc

$Mg_{(s)} + Zn^{2+}_{(aq)} \rightarrow$ .... $+ Zn_{(s)}$

OXIDATION
Mg → ....

REDUCTION
$Zn^{2+} + 2e^- \rightarrow$ ....

This is a .... reaction.

The .... ions are spectator ions (they don't ....), so they aren't .... in the equation.

Topic 4 — Chemical Changes

Second Go: ...../...../.....

Redox Reactions and Ionic Equations

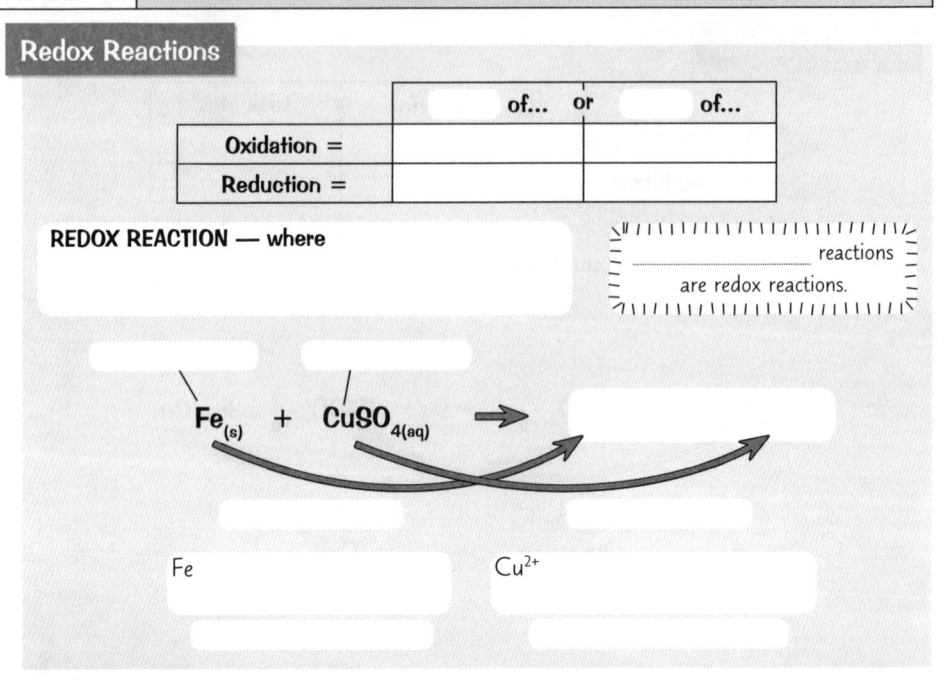

Redox Reactions

		_____ of... or _____ of...
Oxidation =		
Reduction =		

REDOX REACTION — where _____

_____ reactions are redox reactions.

$Fe_{(s)}$ + $CuSO_{4(aq)}$ → _____

Fe Cu^{2+}

Ionic Equations

IONIC EQUATIONS only show _____.

magnesium + ... → .... + zinc

This is a _____.

$Mg_{(s)}$ + $Zn^{2+}_{(aq)}$ → _____

OXIDATION   REDUCTION

Topic 4 — Chemical Changes

Electrolysis

First Go: ..... /..... /.....

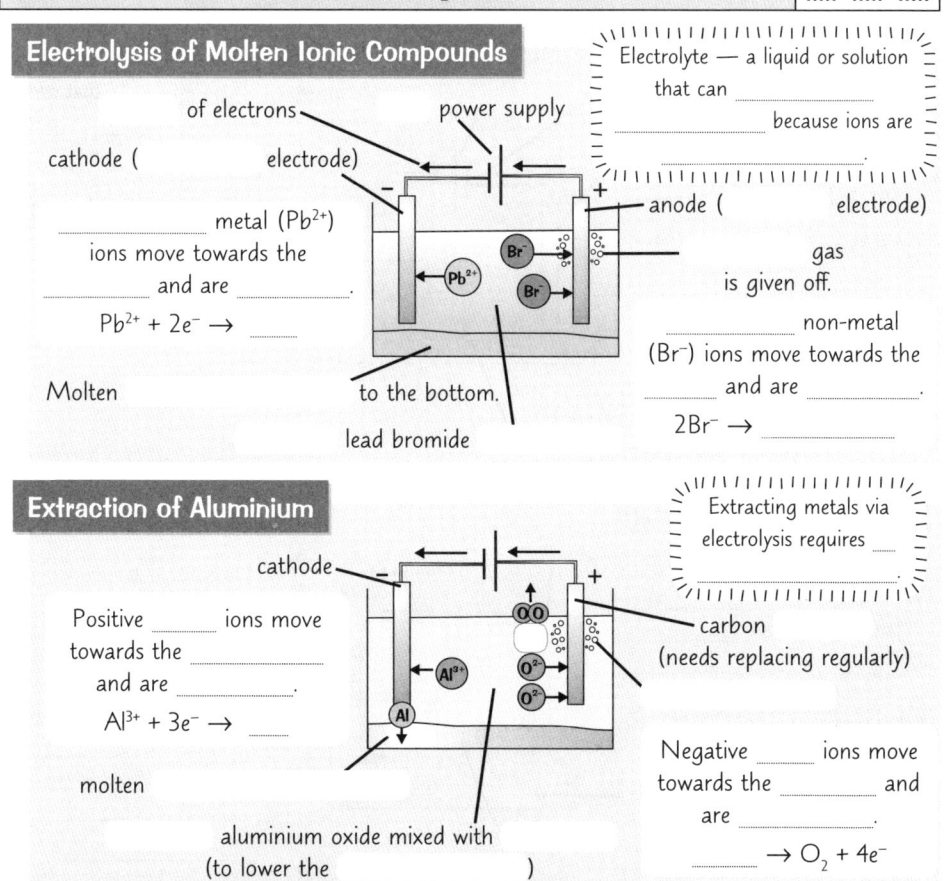

Electrolysis of Molten Ionic Compounds

Electrolyte — a liquid or solution that can .... because ions are ....

- of electrons
- power supply
- cathode (............ electrode)
- .... metal (Pb^{2+}) ions move towards the .... and are ....
- $Pb^{2+} + 2e^- \rightarrow$ ....
- Molten .... to the bottom.
- lead bromide
- anode (............ electrode)
- .... gas is given off.
- .... non-metal (Br^-) ions move towards the .... and are ....
- $2Br^- \rightarrow$ ....

Extraction of Aluminium

Extracting metals via electrolysis requires ....

- cathode
- Positive .... ions move towards the .... and are ....
- $Al^{3+} + 3e^- \rightarrow$ ....
- molten ....
- aluminium oxide mixed with .... (to lower the ....)
- carbon .... (needs replacing regularly)
- Negative .... ions move towards the .... and are ....
- .... $\rightarrow O_2 + 4e^-$

Electrolysis of Aqueous Ionic Compounds

$CuSO_4$ solution

NaCl solution

.... produced at anode if .... are present.

.... produced at cathode if metal is more .... H_2.

.... produced at .... if it is .... than H_2.

.... produced at anode if .... are present.

$4OH^- \rightarrow$ .... $+ 4e^-$

$2H^+ + 2e^- \rightarrow$ ....

Topic 4 — Chemical Changes

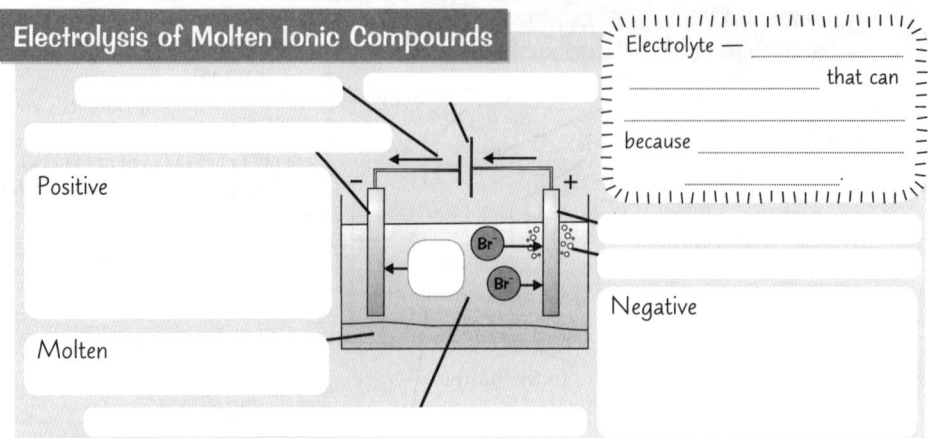

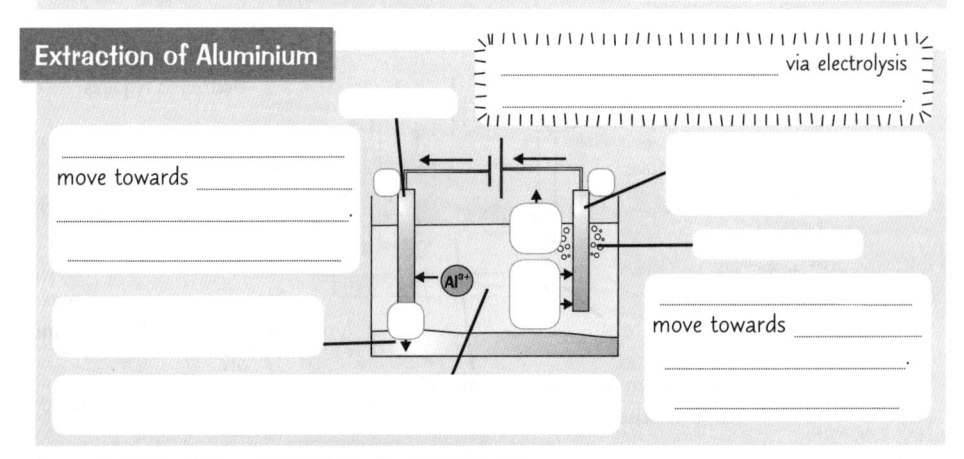

Second Go: ...../...../.....

Electrolysis

Electrolysis of Molten Ionic Compounds

Positive

Molten

Electrolyte — .... that can ....
because ....
....

Extraction of Aluminium

move towards ....
....

.... via electrolysis
....

move towards ....
....

Electrolysis of Aqueous Ionic Compounds

$CuSO_4$ solution

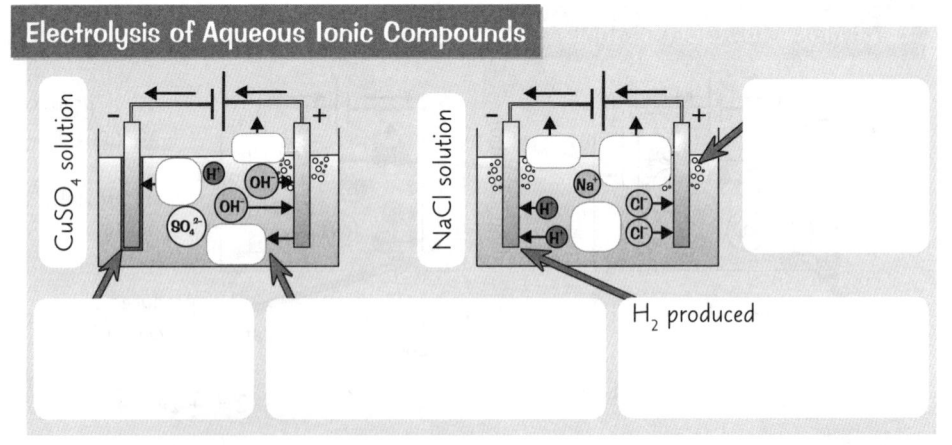

NaCl solution

Negative

H_2 produced

Topic 4 — Chemical Changes

Mixed Practice Quizzes

Here are some quick-fire quiz questions to test what you've done on p.59-68.
No, honestly, you're welcome. Mark each test yourself and tot up your score.

Quiz 1   Date: ...... / ...... / ......

1) What name is given to a base that is soluble in water?
2) What ions are produced when an acid ionises in water?
3) Give an example of a weak acid.
4) What type of acid completely ionises in water?
5) How is a reactive metal such as potassium extracted from a compound?
6) What is produced when a metal reacts with water?
7) Is oxidation the gain or loss of electrons?
8) Why are spectator ions not shown in an ionic equation?
9) Explain what is meant by the term 'electrolyte'.
10) What is produced at the anode during the extraction of aluminium?

Total:

Quiz 2   Date: ...... / ...... / ......

1) What is the pH of a neutral solution?
2) Give two ways of measuring the pH of a solution.
3) What is produced by the reaction of an acid and a metal oxide?
4) Define a weak acid.
5) How does increasing the acid concentration affect the pH of a solution?
6) True or false? Unreactive metals readily form positive ions.
7) True or false? The reaction between lithium and cold dilute acid is moderate.
8) What occurs in a redox reaction?
9) What name is given to the negative electrode in electrolysis?
10) What material is used to make the anode in aluminium extraction?

Total:

Topic 4 — Chemical Changes

Mixed Practice Quizzes

Quiz 3 — Date: ...... / ...... / ......

1) True or false? Universal indicator gives an exact pH value.
2) Which ions react in a neutralisation reaction between an acid and a base?
3) Which type of salt is produced when HNO_3 reacts with a metal carbonate?
4) What is pH a measure of?
5) What is acid strength a measure of?
6) How is iron extracted from iron oxide?
7) Describe what occurs during a displacement reaction.
8) Is reduction the gain or loss of oxygen?
9) What is produced at the cathode during the electrolysis of molten lead bromide?
10) What determines whether hydrogen gas is produced at the cathode during the electrolysis of an aqueous ionic compound?

Total:

Quiz 4 — Date: ...... / ...... / ......

1) Give a method of producing soluble salts.
2) What method could you use to find out the exact volume of acid required to neutralise a quantity of alkali?
3) What can be reacted with an acid to produce carbon dioxide?
4) Give an example of a strong acid.
5) True or false? Calcium is less reactive than zinc.
6) Name a metal that does not react with either acid or water.
7) Give an example of a redox reaction.
8) Give the anode half-equation for the electrolysis of lead bromide.
9) What is mixed with molten aluminium oxide to lower the melting point?
10) What substances are produced at the anode during the electrolysis of an aqueous ionic compound if no halide ions are present?

Total:

Topic 4 — Chemical Changes

Topic 5 — Energy Changes

Endothermic & Exothermic Reactions

First Go: ..... / ..... / .....

Energy Transfer

Energy is _____ in chemical reactions. After a reaction, the _____ amount of energy in the universe is _____.

ENDOTHERMIC reaction:
_____ energy from the surroundings — shown by a _____ in temperature.
Reactions include:
•
• Citric acid + sodium hydrogencarbonate
Use: some _____ packs

EXOTHERMIC reaction:
_____ energy to the surroundings — shown by a _____ in temperature.
Reactions include:
•
• Most _____
• Neutralisation reactions
Uses: self-heating cans and hand warmers

Reaction Profiles

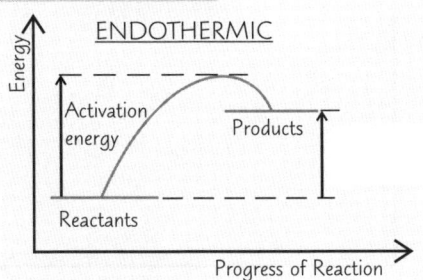

ENDOTHERMIC
(Energy vs Progress of Reaction graph with Activation energy, Reactants, Products labelled)

(Exothermic graph with Activation energy labelled)

ACTIVATION ENERGY (E_a) — _____ of energy that reactants _____.

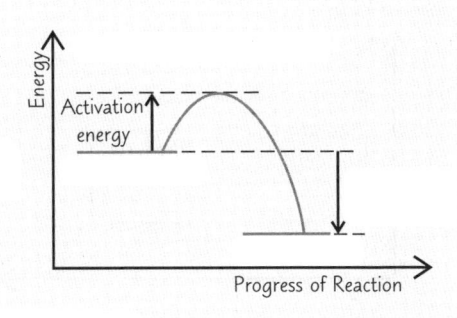

Bond Energies

BOND _____ — ENDOTHERMIC

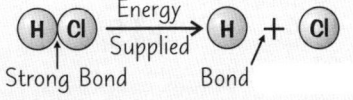

(H)(Cl) →[Energy Supplied] (H) + (Cl)
Strong Bond   Bond

Endothermic reactions: energy used to _____ than the energy released by _____.

BOND _____ — EXOTHERMIC

(C) + (O) → (C)(O) + Energy Released
              Strong Bond

Exothermic reactions: energy released by _____ than the energy used to _____.

overall energy change = _____ energy needed to _____ − _____ energy released by _____

These energies can be calculated from _____

Topic 5 — Energy Changes

Endothermic & Exothermic Reactions

Second Go:
..... / ..... / .....

Energy Transfer

Energy is _____. After a reaction, the _____.

_____ reaction:
Takes in energy

EXOTHERMIC reaction:
Transfers energy

Reactions include:

Reactions include:

Uses: self-heating cans and

Use: some

Reaction Profiles

ENDOTHERMIC
(graph with Activation energy, Reactants, Products)

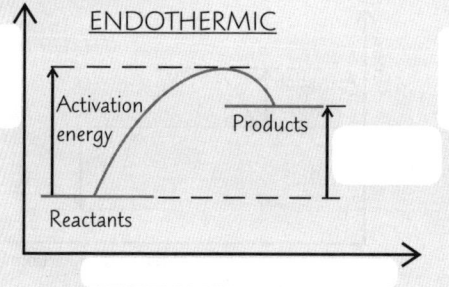

ACTIVATION ENERGY (E_a) —

Bond Energies

_____ — ENDOTHERMIC

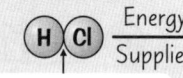

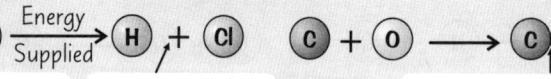

$H-Cl \xrightarrow{Energy\ Supplied} H + Cl$ $C + O \longrightarrow C-O +$

Endothermic reactions: energy used to

Exothermic reactions: energy released by

⬅ These energies

_____ = _____ − _____

Topic 5 — Energy Changes

Cells, Batteries and Fuel Cells

First Go: ..... /..... /.....

Cells and Batteries

Electrochemical cells use _____ to produce _____.

simple _____

wire (allows the _____ to flow)

_____ the _____ (measures _____ of the cell)

Reactions between _____

set up a _____ _____ (usually metals)

between the _____.

The type of _____ used will both affect the _____.

BATTERY — _____ cells connected in _____.

E.g. _____ batteries are non-rechargeable.

Voltages of the _____ in the battery are _____.

Non-rechargeable cells and batteries	Rechargeable cells and batteries
Reaction in cell is _____ — _____ once one reactant is _____.	Reaction in cell is reversible — the cell can be _____ by connecting it to an _____, reversing the reaction.

Hydrogen Fuel Cells

A fuel cell uses the electrochemical _____ of a fuel (e.g. _____) to produce a _____.

Electrical current — the _____ of _____ electrons through the _____ circuit.

_____ in

oxygen in O_2

(−ve electrode)

(+ve electrode)

H_2O → water and heat out

Anode reaction (oxidation):
_____ → _____ + $2e^-$

Cathode reaction (reduction):
$O_2 + 4H^+ + 4e^- →$ _____

The overall equation is: _____

Advantages of hydrogen fuel cells compared with batteries	Disadvantages of hydrogen fuel cells compared with batteries
Less _____ over cell's lifetime.	Storage of H_2 gas takes up _____.
Don't need recharging/replacing as _____.	H_2 production can _____ greenhouse gases.
_____ to make.	H_2 is _____ — hard to store safely.

Topic 5 — Energy Changes

Cells, Batteries and Fuel Cells

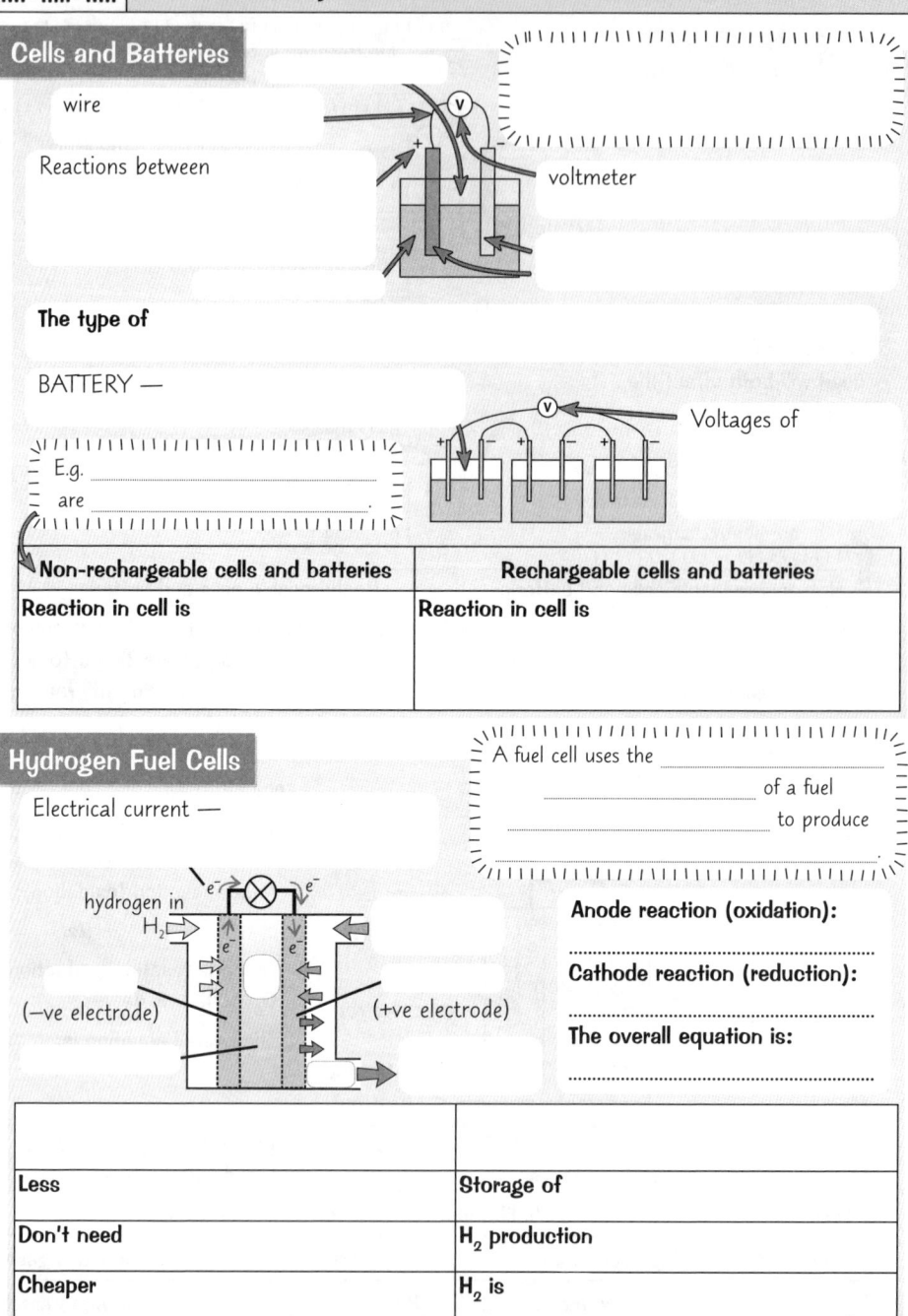

Second Go: ...../...../......

Cells and Batteries

wire _____

Reactions between _____

voltmeter

The type of _____

BATTERY — _____

E.g. _____
are _____ .

Voltages of _____

Non-rechargeable cells and batteries	Rechargeable cells and batteries
Reaction in cell is	Reaction in cell is

Hydrogen Fuel Cells

Electrical current — _____

A fuel cell uses the _____ of a fuel _____ to produce _____ .

(−ve electrode)   (+ve electrode)

Anode reaction (oxidation): _____

Cathode reaction (reduction): _____

The overall equation is: _____

Less	Storage of
Don't need	H_2 production
Cheaper	H_2 is

Topic 5 — Energy Changes

Mixed Practice Quizzes

Just a quick little section, that one. Keep up the good work by having a go at these questions, all based on the information on p.71-74.

Quiz 1   Date: ...... / ...... / ......

1) What type of reaction takes in energy from the surroundings?
2) What is meant by the term 'activation energy'?
3) True or false? Forming new bonds is an endothermic process.
4) Are alkaline batteries rechargeable?
5) True or false? Some sports injury packs use endothermic reactions.
6) What is formed when two or more cells are connected in series?
7) Give an example of an endothermic reaction.
8) What is the product of the reaction that takes place in a hydrogen fuel cell?
9) Give one problem associated with the storage of H_2 gas for use in fuel cells.
10) How is the energy released by an exothermic reaction shown on a reaction profile?

Total:

Quiz 2   Date: ...... / ...... / ......

1) Does the overall energy of the universe change after a reaction?
2) Give an example of a product that uses an exothermic reaction.
3) In the reaction profile for an endothermic reaction, are the reactants or products at higher energy?
4) What name is given to the positive electrode in a fuel cell?
5) True or false? In exothermic reactions, more energy is released to form bonds than is used to break bonds.
6) What type of material are the electrodes in a cell usually made from?
7) True or false? The reaction in non-rechargeable cells is reversible.
8) What is the half-equation for the anode reaction in a hydrogen fuel cell?
9) Is fuel in a fuel cell electrochemically oxidised or reduced?
10) What can the total energy needed to break bonds in a reaction be calculated from?

Total:

Topic 5 — Energy Changes

Mixed Practice Quizzes

Quiz 3 Date: ...... / ...... / ......

1) Does an endothermic reaction transfer energy to or from the surroundings?
2) True or false? In a hydrogen fuel cell, hydrogen is reduced.
3) Which produces less pollution over its lifetime — a fuel cell or a battery?
4) What type of reaction requires more energy to break bonds than is released in forming new ones?
5) Give two factors that affect the size of the voltage of a cell.
6) How can a rechargeable cell be recharged?
7) Would you observe an increase or a decrease in the temperature of the surroundings in an exothermic reaction?
8) True or false? A simple cell is made up of an electrolyte and two identical electrodes.
9) Give two examples of types of reaction that are exothermic.
10) Give the half-equation for the cathode reaction in a hydrogen fuel cell.

Total:

Quiz 4 Date: ...... / ...... / ......

1) In which type of reaction does the temperature of the surroundings fall?
2) True or false? In an exothermic reaction profile, the products are at a lower energy than the reactants.
3) What's the minimum amount of energy that reactants need to react called?
4) What is represented on the horizontal axis of a reaction profile?
5) True or false? The voltage provided by a battery is the combined voltage of each cell in the battery.
6) Give a formula for calculating the overall energy change of a reaction.
7) What is the minimum number of cells required to create a battery?
8) What are the two reactants in a hydrogen fuel cell?
9) How is the energy absorbed by an endothermic reaction shown on a reaction profile?
10) Give one problem associated with the production of H_2 for fuel cells.

Total:

Topic 5 — Energy Changes

Topic 6 — The Rate and Extent of Chemical Change

Rates of Reaction

First Go:
...../...../.....

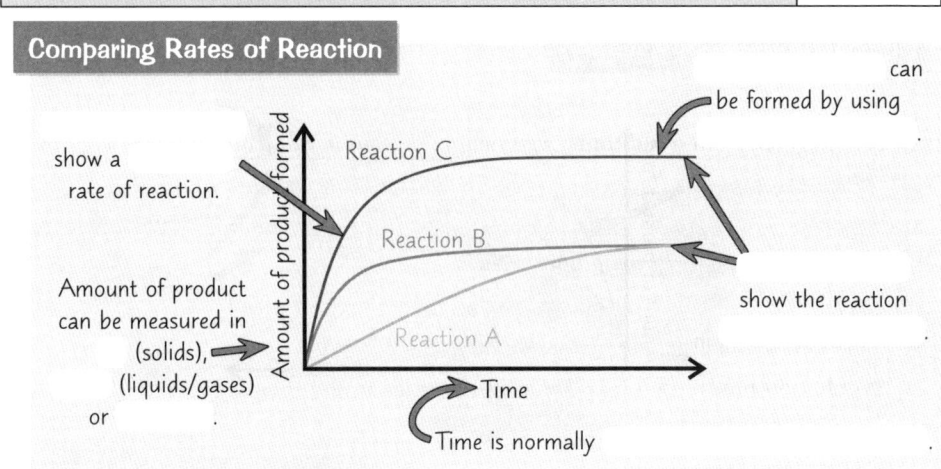

Comparing Rates of Reaction

_____ can be formed by using _____.

_____ show a rate of reaction.

_____ show the reaction _____.

Amount of product can be measured in _____ (solids), _____ (liquids/gases) or _____.

Time is normally _____.

(Graph: Amount of product formed vs Time, showing Reaction C, Reaction B, Reaction A)

Measuring Rates of Reaction

$$\text{Mean rate of reaction} = \frac{\text{_____}}{\text{Time}} \text{ or } \frac{\text{_____}}{\text{Time}}$$

Units depend on _____ — they're in the form _____.

Three common _____ : _____ g/s _____ mol/s

Using Rate Graphs

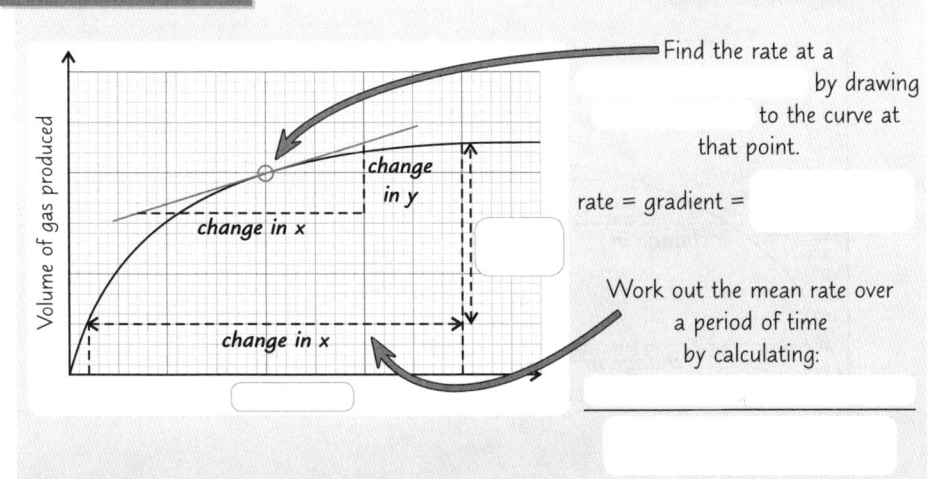

Find the rate at a _____ by drawing _____ to the curve at that point.

rate = gradient = _____

Work out the mean rate over a period of time _____ by calculating:

_____

(Graph: Volume of gas produced vs time, showing change in y / change in x)

Rates of Reaction

Second Go: ...../...../.....

Comparing Rates of Reaction

[blank box]

can be measured in

[blank box]

.

Graph: Amount of product formed vs time, showing Reaction C (fastest, highest), Reaction B (middle), Reaction A (slowest)

Measuring Rates of Reaction

Mean rate of reaction = ──────────── or ────────────

Units depend on   .
— they're in the form   :

Using Rate Graphs

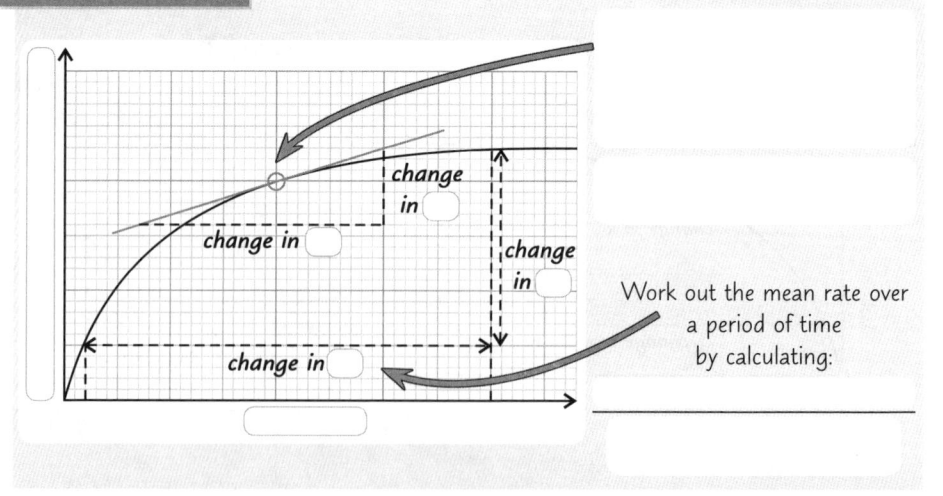

Graph with tangent line at a point, showing change in [ ] / change in [ ], and change in [ ] / change in [ ]

Work out the mean rate over a period of time by calculating:

───────────────

Topic 6 — The Rate and Extent of Chemical Change

Factors Affecting Rates of Reaction

First Go: ..../..../....

Collision Theory

The minimum energy particles need to react is called the _____.

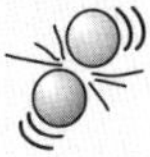

High
High
Fast

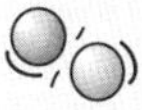

Low
Low
Slow

The rate of a chemical reaction depends on...

Collision frequency — the _____ between particles, the _____ the rate of reaction. So doubling the frequency of _____ would _____ the rate.

Collision energy — _____ energy needs to be transferred in a collision to overcome the _____ and _____ to start the reaction.

Temperature

Particles _____ more _____ and collide with more energy.

Cold   Hot

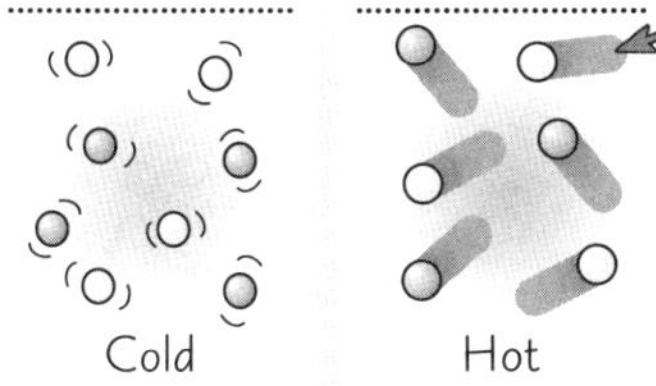

Pressure or Concentration

_____ in the same _____ — more frequent _____

SLOW RATE   FAST RATE

Low pressure/concentration   High pressure/concentration

Surface Area

_____ for particles to _____ with — more collisions.

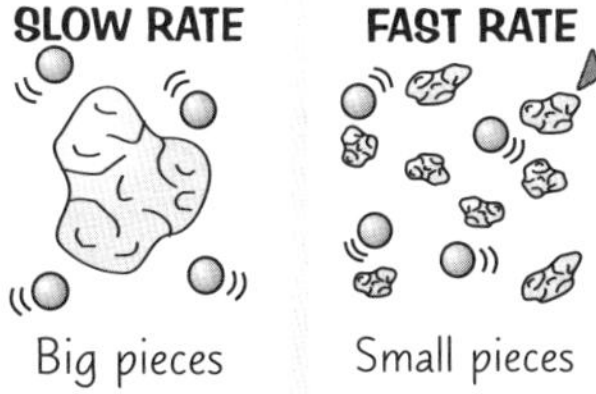

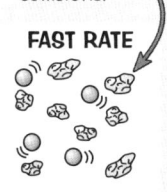

SLOW RATE   FAST RATE

Big pieces   Small pieces

The _____ the piece of solid, the larger the _____ _____ ratio.

Catalysts

CATALYSTS — _____ reactions without being used up by providing an _____ for the reaction. Different reactions need _____.

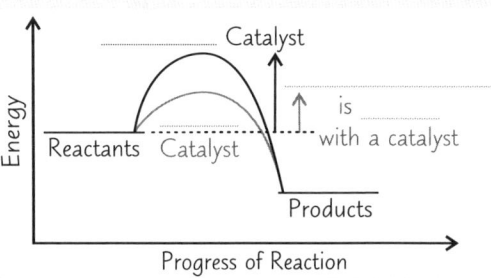

Energy
Reactants   Catalyst   Catalyst
                              ↑ is _____
                              with a catalyst
                         Products

Progress of Reaction

Enzymes are _____ catalysts.

Topic 6 — The Rate and Extent of Chemical Change

Factors Affecting Rates of Reaction

Second Go: ..... / ..... / .....

Collision Theory

The minimum energy particles need to react is called the ....

The rate of a chemical reaction depends on...

Collision frequency —

Collision energy —

Temperature

Pressure or Concentration

.... in the same .... — more frequent

Low .... / High .... /

Surface Area

The ...., the ...., ...

Catalysts

CATALYSTS —

.... is .... with a catalyst

Energy vs Progress of Reaction
Reactants → Catalyst → Products

Enzymes are .... catalysts.

Topic 6 — The Rate and Extent of Chemical Change

Reversible Reactions

First Go: ...../...../.....

Equilibrium

Equilibrium can only be reached when a .... takes place in a .... (where nothing can enter or leave).

$A + B \rightleftharpoons C + D$

.... where the products can react to form ....

At equilibrium, the .... of reactants and products ....

Forward Reaction: A, B → C, D
Same rate
Backward Reaction: C, D → A, B

....................: the equilibrium lies to the ....

....................: the equilibrium lies to the ....

Changing reaction conditions can change the ....

.... the reaction favours the left. ammonium chloride $\rightleftharpoons$ ammonia + hydrogen chloride .... the reaction favours the right.

Exothermic and Endothermic Reactions

If the reaction is .... in one direction, it will be .... in the other.

Hydrated copper sulfate $\rightleftharpoons$ Anhydrous copper sulfate + Water

The .... is transferred in each direction.

Le Chatelier's Principle

If the .... of a reversible reaction are changed, the system tries to ....

		The equilibrium shifts to favour the...
....	increases	.... direction to take in heat energy.
	decreases	...exothermic direction to .... heat energy.
Pressure	increases	...side with fewer molecules of gas to .... the pressure.
	decreases	...side with more .... the pressure.

If .... of a .... is changed, the system will respond to ....

If the concentration of...	The system responds to...
....	...make more products.
...reactants	...make more ....

Topic 6 — The Rate and Extent of Chemical Change

Reversible Reactions

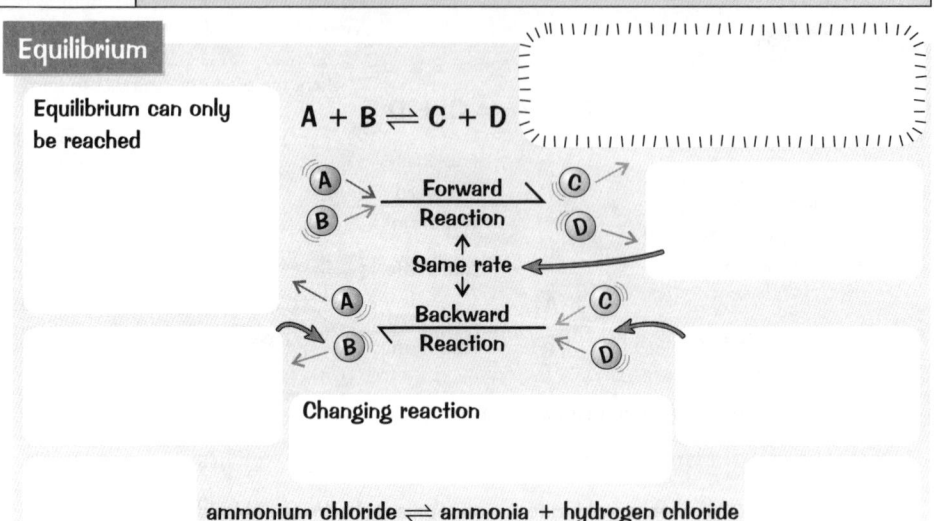

Second Go: ..../..../....

Equilibrium

Equilibrium can only be reached

$$A + B \rightleftharpoons C + D$$

Forward Reaction
Same rate
Backward Reaction

Changing reaction

ammonium chloride $\rightleftharpoons$ ammonia + hydrogen chloride

Exothermic and Endothermic Reactions

If the reaction is

Hydrated copper sulfate $\rightleftharpoons$ Anhydrous copper sulfate + Water

Le Chatelier's Principle

If .... are changed, the system tries to ....

		The equilibrium shifts to favour the...
....	increases	.... direction to ....
	decreases	.... direction to ....
....	increases	...side with .... molecules of gas ....
	decreases	...side with .... molecules of gas ....

If .... of a .... is changed, the system will respond to ....

If the concentration of...	The system responds to...
...	...make ....
...	...make ....

Topic 6 — The Rate and Extent of Chemical Change

Mixed Practice Quizzes

Time to increase your rate of revision by throwing in a quiz catalyst. All of these questions are based on p.77-82, so make sure you've gone over those first.

Quiz 1   Date: ...... / ...... / ......

1) Can a reversible reaction be endothermic in both directions?
2) How does heating a substance affect the movement of its particles?
3) How will equilibrium shift if the pressure of a reversible reaction between gases is lowered?
4) How can you tell from a rate graph when a reaction is finished?
5) True or false? Units of rate are always in the form amount/mass.
6) What effect will doubling the collision frequency have on the rate?
7) How does breaking a solid into smaller pieces affect its surface area?
8) How does a catalyst affect the activation energy of a reaction?
9) True or false? The steeper the line on a rate graph, the faster the reaction.
10) How would you find the rate at a specific point on a rate graph?

Total:

Quiz 2   Date: ...... / ...... / ......

1) What does it mean if a reaction is reversible?
2) What is represented by the horizontal axis on a rate graph?
3) How does decreasing the concentration of reactants in solution affect the rate of reaction?
4) What are biological catalysts called?
5) True or false? The concentrations of reactants don't change at equilibrium.
6) Give one way of increasing the collision frequency of particles in a reaction.
7) True or false? All reactions can use the same catalysts.
8) According to collision theory, which two factors determine the rate of a reaction?
9) Give the equation for calculating a mean rate of reaction from the amount of product formed and the time taken.
10) How would increasing the concentration of reactants affect an equilibrium?

Total:

Topic 6 — The Rate and Extent of Chemical Change

Mixed Practice Quizzes

Quiz 3 Date: ...... / ...... / ......

1) True or false? Equilibrium can be only reached in an open system.
2) What is the activation energy of a reaction?
3) How does increasing the concentration of the particles in a reaction affect the collision frequency?
4) How would you work out the mean rate of reaction over a period of time?
5) What would the units of rate be if the amount of product formed was measured in cm^3 and the time taken was measured in seconds?
6) How can you tell which reaction shown on a single graph has the fastest rate?
7) Why does increasing the surface area of a reactant increase reaction rate?
8) What can you say about the rates of the forward and backward reactions of a reversible reaction at equilibrium?
9) How do catalysts speed up reactions?
10) True or false? Increasing collision frequency, increases rate of reaction.

Total:

Quiz 4 Date: ...... / ...... / ......

1) True or false? A catalyst is used up in a reaction.
2) What is meant by a closed system?
3) In which direction will an equilibrium shift in response to an increase in temperature?
4) True or false? Mean rate of reaction = amount of reactant used × time
5) Why does a higher pressure mean a faster rate of reaction between gases?
6) What is the minimum amount of collision energy needed to start a reaction called?
7) If the equilibrium lies to the left, are there more reactants or products?
8) True or false? Lowering the temperature of a reaction means the average energy of colliding particles increases.
9) Which factor affects both collision frequency and collision energy?
10) State Le Chatelier's Principle.

Total:

Topic 6 — The Rate and Extent of Chemical Change

Topic 7 — Organic Chemistry

Crude Oil and Fractional Distillation

First Go: ..... /..... /.....

Crude Oil

CRUDE OIL — a mixture of many _____.

_____ are formed from only hydrogen and carbon atoms.

It's a finite resource found in _____ and formed from _____ that have spent _____ buried in mud.

Crude oil is processed to produce _____ and to provide stock chemicals used _____ polymers, _____, lubricants etc.

Combustion

COMPLETE COMBUSTION — an _____ reaction that occurs when a _____ reacts with plenty of _____.

hydrocarbon + _____ ↓
_____ + _____

Hydrocarbons are used as _____ because combustion _____ a lot of energy.

Hydrocarbons

As the length of the hydrocarbon chain increases, the...	
...boiling point	.
...	increases.
...flammability	.

Fractional Distillation

FRACTIONAL DISTILLATION — a process used to _____ the _____ in crude oil into _____ according to _____.

Shorter hydrocarbons have _____ so condense near the _____ of the column.

→ LPG (_____)

COOL

Crude oil is _____ until most has _____.

→ diesel oil

→ heavy fuel oil

crude oil →

VERY HOT

Longer hydrocarbons have _____ so condense near the _____ of the column.

Crude Oil and Fractional Distillation

Second Go: ..... / ..... / .....

Crude Oil

CRUDE OIL —

.... only contain ....

It's a finite resource

Crude oil is processed to ....
.... used to manufacture ....,
...................................., lubricants etc.

Combustion

COMPLETE COMBUSTION —

.... + ...
↓
.... + ...

Hydrocarbons are used as ....

Hydrocarbons

As the length of the .... , the...

Fractional Distillation

FRACTIONAL DISTILLATION —

Shorter hydrocarbons

COOL

Crude oil is

Longer hydrocarbons

VERY HOT

Topic 7 — Organic Chemistry

Alkanes and Cracking

First Go: ..... /..... /.....

Alkanes

ALKANES — the only .... type of hydrocarbon, containing .... (they're saturated).

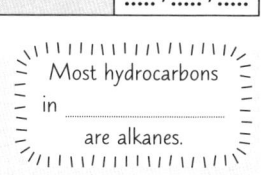

Most hydrocarbons in .... are alkanes.

The general formula for the .... of alkanes is ....

Number of carbon atoms	1	2	3	4
Name	Methane		Propane	
Formula		C_2H_6	C_3H_8	

Structure		H H
		  | |
		H—C—C—H
		  | |
		H H
				H H H H
				  | | | |
				H—C—C—C—C—H
				  | | | |
				H H H H

Two Methods of Cracking

There is .... for fuels with .... carbon chains.

CRACKING — breaks down .... hydrocarbons into ....

.... -chain alkane ⟹ .... + alkene

Alkenes are used to make .... and are .... for making other chemicals.

Long-chain hydrocarbons are .... by heating.

Hydrocarbon vapour is passed over a ....

Hydrocarbon vapour is mixed with .... and heated to ....

① .... cracking

② .... cracking

Topic 7 — Organic Chemistry

Alkanes and Cracking

Second Go: ...../...../.....

Alkanes

ALKANES —

The _____ for the _____.

Most hydrocarbons _____.

Number of carbon atoms	1	2	3	4
Name				
Formula				
Structure				

Two Methods of Cracking

There is _____ for fuels with _____.

CRACKING — _____

_____ → _____ + _____

Alkenes are used _____.

_____ hydrocarbons are _____.

Hydrocarbon vapour is _____   Hydrocarbon vapour is _____

(1) _____   (2) _____

Topic 7 — Organic Chemistry

Alkenes and their Reactions

First Go: ..... /..... /.....

Alkenes

ALKENES — _____ hydrocarbons that have a carbon-carbon _____ (this is the _____).

Functional group — a group of atoms in _____ that dictate how _____.

The _____ double bond makes them _____ than alkanes.

The general formula for the alkenes is _____.

Number of carbon atoms	2	3	4	5
Name		Propene		Pentene
Formula	C_2H_4	C_3H_6		
Structure			e.g. H-C-C-C=C with H atoms	e.g. H-C-C-C-C=C with H atoms

Incomplete Combustion

INCOMPLETE COMBUSTION — when a fuel _____ but there's _____ to burn completely.

Alkenes produce a _____ when they combust incompletely.

alkene + _____ → _____ + _____ + carbon dioxide + water

Addition Reactions

H_2O reacts as _____.

R-C(H)(H)-C(H)(H)-H ← catalyst — C=C (with R, H, H, H) — + H_2O catalyst → alcohol

The atoms add _____ the C=C bond.

↓

H Br
R-C-C-H
Br H
halogenoalkane

Cl_2 and I_2 react _____.

Adding an alkene to _____ causes it to change from _____.

bromine test

Topic 7 — Organic Chemistry

Alkenes and their Reactions

Second Go: ..../..../....

Alkenes

ALKENES —

The _____ makes them _____.

— a group of atoms in _____

The general formula for _____.

Number of carbon atoms	2	3	4	5
Name				
Formula				
Structure			e.g.	e.g.

Incomplete Combustion

INCOMPLETE COMBUSTION —

Alkenes produce _____ when _____.

→

Addition Reactions

_____ reacts as _____.

R\C=C/H (with H on bottom both sides), catalyst

The atoms _____

_____ react in _____.

H Br
R—C—C—H
Br H

Adding an alkene

Topic 7 — Organic Chemistry

Mixed Practice Quizzes

Hopefully you've cracked all the information on p.85-90, because it's time for some questions. Remember to check how you've done afterwards.

Quiz 1 — Date: ...... / ...... / ......

1) What type of molecules is crude oil mostly made up of?
2) What is the chemical formula of butene?
3) Which are more reactive — alkanes or alkenes?
4) Give two examples of products that are made from chemicals produced from crude oil.
5) Why are hydrocarbons used as fuels?
6) What is the purpose of cracking hydrocarbons?
7) What is the general formula for alkenes?
8) Give the product of the reaction between an alkene and hydrogen.
9) Describe how the atoms in an addition reaction add to the alkene, relative to the C=C double bond.
10) Name two methods of cracking.

Total:

Quiz 2 — Date: ...... / ...... / ......

1) What happens to crude oil during fractional distillation?
2) Which two elements make up hydrocarbons?
3) What type of flame does an alkene produce when it combusts incompletely?
4) True or false? When an alkane is cracked, only alkenes are produced.
5) What is the functional group in an alkene?
6) What would you see if you added an alkene to bromine water?
7) How is the length of the hydrocarbon chain related to viscosity?
8) What are the products of complete combustion of a hydrocarbon fuel?
9) Give three fuels produced from the fractional distillation of crude oil.
10) Where do shorter hydrocarbons condense in a fractionating column?

Total:

Topic 7 — Organic Chemistry

Mixed Practice Quizzes

Quiz 3 Date: ...... / ...... / ......

1) Are long-chain hydrocarbons more flammable than short-chain hydrocarbons?
2) What is used as the catalyst in catalytic cracking?
3) What is the chemical formula of methane?
4) How many carbon atoms are present in a molecule of propene?
5) What did crude oil form from?
6) True or false? Fractionating columns are hotter at the top than the bottom.
7) What is meant by an unsaturated hydrocarbon?
8) What is reacted with an alkene to produce an alcohol?
9) Give one use of alkenes.
10) What causes a fuel to undergo incomplete combustion?

Total:

Quiz 4 Date: ...... / ...... / ......

1) What is the formula of ethene?
2) What type of reaction produces a halogenoalkane from an alkene and bromine?
3) Where is crude oil found?
4) What is the general formula for alkanes?
5) How many hydrogen atoms are present in a 3-carbon alkane?
6) Are alkanes saturated or unsaturated?
7) What is a functional group?
8) How are long-chain hydrocarbons vaporised before cracking?
9) Does a saturated compound contain any carbon-carbon double bonds?
10) How does the chain length of a hydrocarbon affect its boiling point?

Total:

Topic 7 — Organic Chemistry

Addition Polymers

First Go: ..... / ..... / .....

Addition Polymerisation

POLYMERS — formed when lots of small molecules
(_____) _____ .

ADDITION POLYMERISATION — when molecules with _____ join together in _____ .

'n' means there can be _____ of monomers.

Monomer

$$n \begin{pmatrix} H \\ | \\ C=C \\ | \\ H \end{pmatrix} \longrightarrow \begin{pmatrix} H & H \\ | & | \\ -C-C- \\ | & | \\ H & H \end{pmatrix}_n$$

Poly(ethene)

Polymers are named after _____ they're formed from.

REPEATING UNIT — the _____ repeating section of _____ . It contains _____ as the monomer because no other products _____ .

Repeating Units

Four steps for drawing _____ :

$$\begin{pmatrix} H & H \\ | & | \\ H-C-C=C \\ | & | \\ H & H & H \end{pmatrix} \longrightarrow \begin{pmatrix} H_3C & H \\ | & | \\ -C-C- \\ | & | \\ H & H \end{pmatrix}_n$$

To draw _____ from _____ , just _____ the method below.

① Draw the _____ and replace the _____ with a _____ .

② Add an extra _____ to each _____ .

③ Add _____ in the same way that they _____ the double bond.

④ Add _____ and ' _____ '.

Topic 7 — Organic Chemistry

Second Go:
..... / ..... / .....

Addition Polymers

Addition Polymerisation

POLYMERS —

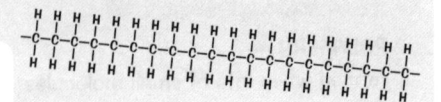

ADDITION POLYMERISATION —

'n' means

$$-n\begin{pmatrix} H & H \\ | & | \\ C=C \\ | & | \\ H & H \end{pmatrix} \longrightarrow$$

Polymers are ....

REPEATING UNIT — the
It contains

Repeating Units

Four steps for .... :

$$n\begin{pmatrix} H & & H \\ | & & | \\ H-C-C=C \\ | & | & | \\ H & H & H \end{pmatrix} \longrightarrow$$

To draw ...., just ....

1. Draw
2. Add
3. Add
4. Add

Topic 7 — Organic Chemistry

Alcohols

First Go:
..... /..... /.....

Alcohols

ALCOHOLS — a compound containing   .

Number of carbon atoms	1	2	3	4
Name	Methanol	Ethanol		
Formula		or	or e.g. $CH_3CH_2CH_2OH$	C_4H_9OH or e.g. $CH_3CH_2CH_2CH_2OH$
Structure	H|H−C−O−H|H		e.g. H−C−C−C−O−H with H H H above and H H H below	

Four Properties of the First Four Alcohols

1. Flammable — they undergo   in air.
   alcohol +   →   +

2. Soluble in water — they give   .

3. They react with sodium to form   .

4. Oxidised by   to form   .

Two key   of alcohols:

       -chain alcohols make good   .   in industry

Fermentation of Alcohols

FERMENTATION — a process where   is used to
                    to aqueous solutions of   .

sugar ⟶   +

Optimum conditions for :		
°C	Slightly solution	conditions

Topic 7 — Organic Chemistry

Second Go: ...../...../.....

Alcohols

Alcohols

ALCOHOLS — _____.

Number of carbon atoms	1	2	3	4
Name				
Formula			or e.g.	or e.g.
Structure			e.g.	e.g.

Four Properties of the First Four Alcohols

① _____ — they undergo _____.

　　　　　_____ + _____ → _____ + _____

② Soluble _____

③ They react _____

④ Oxidised _____

Two key uses of alcohols: [_____] [_____]

Fermentation of Alcohols

FERMENTATION — _____

　　　_____ → _____ + _____

Optimum conditions for fermentation:		

Topic 7 — Organic Chemistry

Carboxylic Acids and Esters

First Go: ..... / ..... / .....

Carboxylic Acids

CARBOXYLIC ACIDS — a compound containing a .... functional group.

Number of carbon atoms	1	2	3	4
Name	Methanoic acid	Ethanoic acid		
Formula		CH_3COOH	C_2H_5COOH	
Structure	H−C(=O)−O−H			H−C(H,H)−C(H,H)−C(H,H)−C(=O)−O−H

Reactions of Carboxylic Acids

Carboxylic acids react like ....

For example:

carboxylic acid + metal ....

↓

.... + carbon dioxide + ...

Properties of Carboxylic Acids

Carboxylic acids are .... — they don't .... when .... in water.

Solution contains both .... and ....

They have a higher .... than .... at the same ....

Esters

ESTERS — molecules formed when .... reacts with ....

.... + ... —acid→ ester + ...

For example:

H−C(H,H)−C(H,H)−O−H + H−C(H,H)−C(=O)−O−H → H−C(H,H)−C(H,H)−O−C(=O)−C(H,H,H) + ...

....

Ethyl ethanoate

Topic 7 — Organic Chemistry

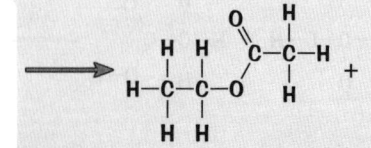

Carboxylic Acids and Esters

Second Go:
..... / ..... / .....

Carboxylic Acids

CARBOXYLIC ACIDS — _____

Number of carbon atoms	1	2	3	4
Name				
Formula				
Structure				

Reactions of Carboxylic Acids

Carboxylic acids _____ _____.

For example:

Properties of Carboxylic Acids

Carboxylic acids _____ —
they don't _____
_____.

_____ contains
both _____
_____.

They have _____

Esters

ESTERS — _____

_____ + _____ → _____ + _____

For example:

_____ → H-C-C-O-C-C-H (ester structure) + _____

Topic 7 — Organic Chemistry

Condensation and Natural Polymers

First Go: ..... / ..... / .....

Condensation Polymers

CONDENSATION POLYMERS — polymers formed from _____ with _____.

In condensation polymerisation, a _____ is _____ for each _____.

Diol   Dicarboxylic acid

n HO—▢—OH + n C(=O)(OH)—▢—C(=O)(OH) ⟶ {—O—▢—O—C(=O)—▢—C(=O)—}_n + 2n _____

▢ = _____

_____ link   Small molecule

functional groups   functional groups

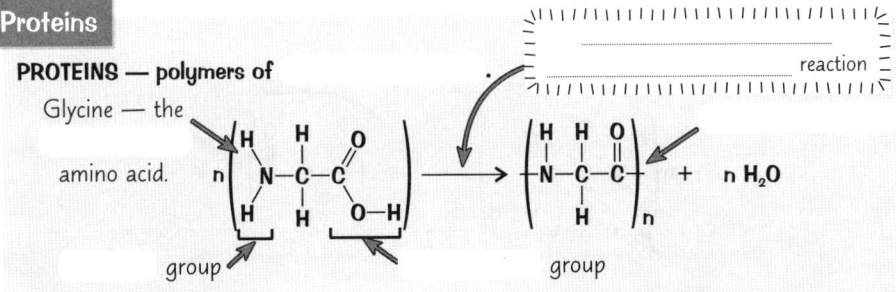

Proteins

PROTEINS — polymers of _____.

Glycine — the _____ amino acid.

n (H₂N—CH₂—COOH) ⟶ (—NH—CH₂—C(=O)—)_n + n H_2O

_____ reaction

_____ group   _____ group

Proteins contain different _____ in their polymer chains, giving them different _____.

DNA

DNA (deoxyribonucleic acid) — a large molecule made up of _____ of _____ nucleotide _____. It is essential to life.

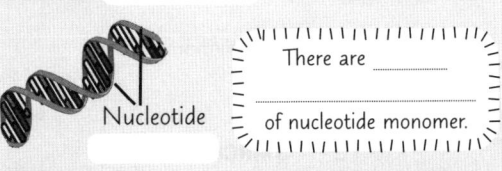

Nucleotide

There are _____ of nucleotide monomer.

DNA encodes _____ information that allows _____ and _____ to develop and _____.

Starch and Cellulose

SUGARS — _____ molecules containing _____.

These monomers can _____ to form large _____, e.g. _____.

STARCH — used by _____ organisms to _____.

CELLULOSE — used to make _____.

Topic 7 — Organic Chemistry

Condensation and Natural Polymers

Condensation Polymers

CONDENSATION POLYMERS —

In condensation polymerisation,

Dicarboxylic acid

Proteins

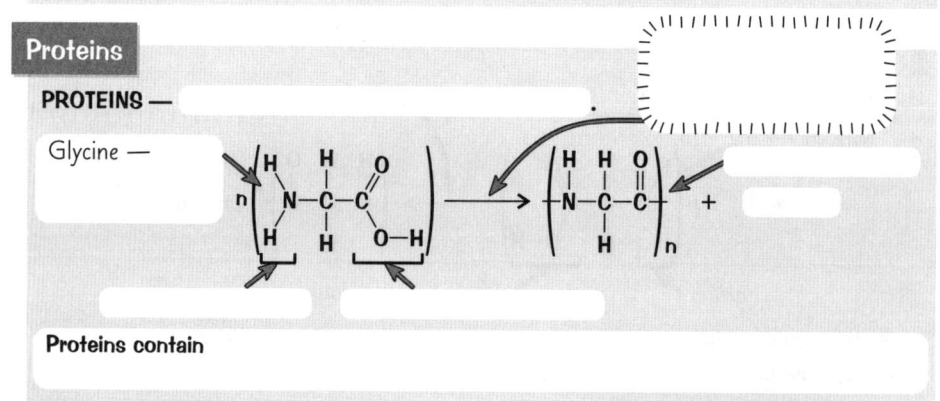

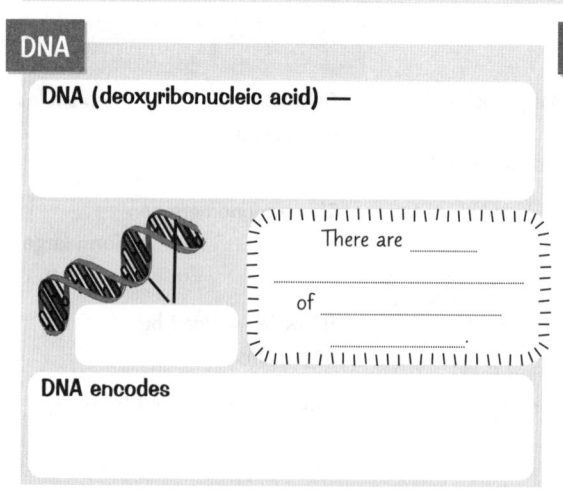

PROTEINS —

Glycine —

Proteins contain

DNA

DNA (deoxyribonucleic acid) —

There are _____ of _____.

DNA encodes

Starch and Cellulose

SUGARS —

These monomers can _____ to form _____, e.g.

STARCH —

CELLULOSE —

Topic 7 — Organic Chemistry

Mixed Practice Quizzes

That's a whole lot of functional groups and interesting reactions. When you're ready, crack on with these quizzes based on everything covered on p.93-100.

Quiz 1 — Date: ...... / ...... / ......

1) What is the functional group of an alcohol?
2) What does DNA stand for?
3) What type of compound is butanoic acid?
4) What is a polymer?
5) What is lost each time a new bond forms in condensation polymerisation?
6) What does 'n' mean in the formula for a polymer?
7) What are the products when an alcohol and a carboxylic acid react in the presence of an acid catalyst?
8) Name one naturally occurring polymer made from sugar monomers.
9) What is the name of the carboxylic acid with two carbon atoms?
10) True or false? The repeating unit of an addition polymer contains the same atoms as the monomer it was formed from.

Total:

Quiz 2 — Date: ...... / ...... / ......

1) What name is given to the small molecules which join together to form a polymer?
2) How many alcohol groups does a diol contain?
3) What monomers join together to form a protein?
4) What gas is produced when an alcohol reacts with sodium?
5) Give the chemical formula for propanol.
6) Give one way that carboxylic acids can be formed from another compound.
7) Give the chemical formula for methanoic acid.
8) Are polypeptides produced by condensation or addition polymerisation?
9) Name the polymer produced from ethene monomers.
10) What feature must molecules have in order to join together to produce an addition polymer?

Total:

Mixed Practice Quizzes

Quiz 3 Date: ...... / ...... / ......

1) Name the ester produced from ethanol and ethanoic acid.
2) What are the optimum conditions for the production of alcohol by fermentation?
3) Give the three products of the reaction between a carboxylic acid and a metal carbonate.
4) Does ethanoic acid have a higher pH than a strong acid such as hydrochloric acid at the same concentration?
5) Is the solution created when an alcohol is dissolved in water acidic, alkaline or neutral?
6) How many products are formed in an addition polymerisation reaction?
7) What products are made when an alcohol undergoes complete combustion?
8) What is the function of DNA?
9) Which alcohol is produced when glucose is fermented by yeast?
10) How many functional groups are present on each monomer in condensation polymerisation?

Total:

Quiz 4 Date: ...... / ...... / ......

1) How many types of nucleotide monomer are there in DNA?
2) State an industrial use of alcohols.
3) Are carboxylic acids strong or weak acids?
4) What type of condensation polymer is formed from a diol and a dicarboxylic acid?
5) What type of polymerisation also produces small molecules such as water?
6) True or false? Carboxylic acids fully ionise when dissolved in water.
7) What is the functional group for carboxylic acids?
8) What are polypeptides polymers of?
9) True or false? Amino acids have only one functional group.
10) How many polymer chains make up a molecule of DNA?

Total:

Topic 7 — Organic Chemistry

Topic 8 — Chemical Analysis

Purity, Formulations and Gas Tests

First Go: ..... / ..... / .....

Purity

	Everyday Definition	Chemical Definition
PURE SUBSTANCE	A substance with .... to it, e.g.	A substance containing .... element .... or ....

A chemically pure substance will:

Melt at a .... at a ....

Impurities in a sample will:
- .... the melting point and .... the melting range.
- .... the boiling point and .... the boiling range.

You can .... the purity of a sample by comparing its .... with that of ....

Formulations

FORMULATIONS — .... mixtures with a ....

Each component in a .... is present in a .... quantity, and .... to the .... of the formulation.

....
cleaning products

....
....

....
cosmetics

paints

....

Four Tests for Gases

1 HYDROGEN burns with a ....

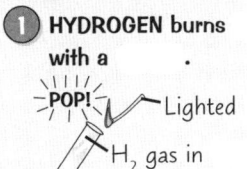

POP! — Lighted ....
H_2 gas in ....

2 OXYGEN will .... a glowing splint.

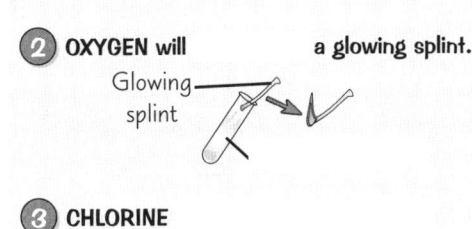

Glowing splint

3 CHLORINE .... litmus paper white.

Litmus paper

4 CARBON DIOXIDE makes limewater turn .... when shaken with or .... it.

Limewater — ....

Topic 8 — Chemical Analysis

Purity, Formulations and Gas Tests

Second Go: ..... / ..... / .....

Purity

	Everyday Definition	Chemical Definition
PURE SUBSTANCE		

A chemically pure substance will:

Impurities in a sample will:

You can .... by comparing ....

Formulations

FORMULATIONS —

Each component in

....
....
....
....
....
....

Four Tests for Gases

1) HYDROGEN

POP!

2) OXYGEN

3) CHLORINE

4) CARBON DIOXIDE

Limewater —

Topic 8 — Chemical Analysis

Paper Chromatography

First Go: ...../...../.....

Two Phases of Chromatography

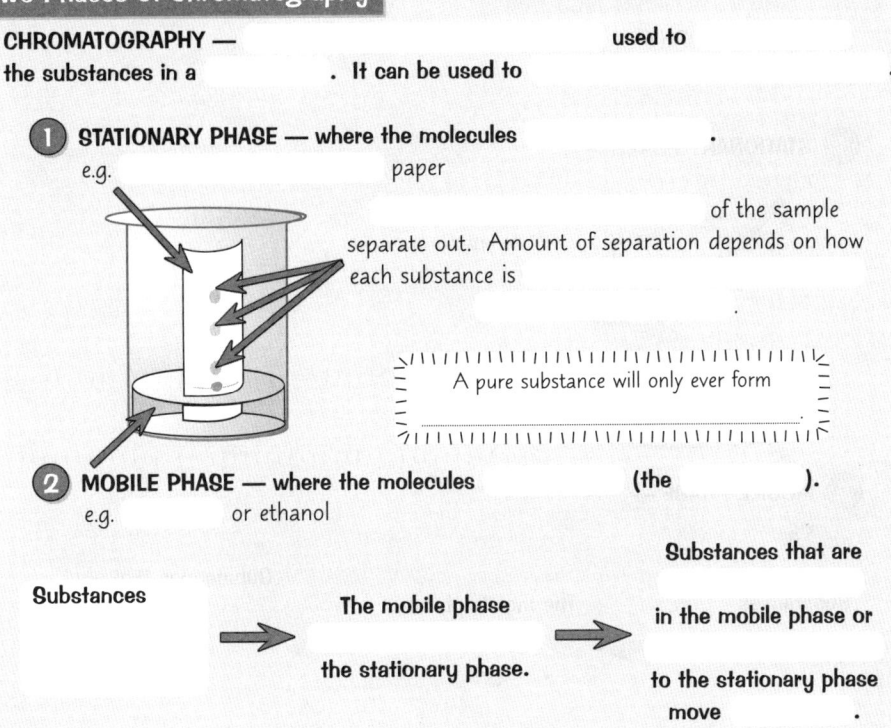

CHROMATOGRAPHY — _____ used to _____ the substances in a _____. It can be used to _____.

① STATIONARY PHASE — where the molecules _____.
e.g. _____ paper

_____ of the sample separate out. Amount of separation depends on how each substance is _____.

> A pure substance will only ever form _____.

② MOBILE PHASE — where the molecules _____ (the _____).
e.g. _____ or ethanol

Substances → The mobile phase _____ the stationary phase. → Substances that are _____ in the mobile phase or _____ to the stationary phase move _____.

R_f Values

R_f VALUE — the _____ between the distance travelled by the _____ and the distance travelled by the _____.

$$R_f = \frac{\text{distance travelled by } \underline{} \text{ (B)}}{\text{distance travelled by } \underline{} \text{ (A)}}$$

Distance moved by _____ (_____)

Spot of _____

_____ (origin)

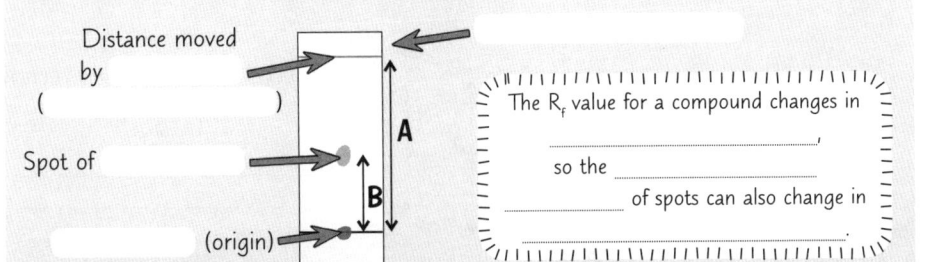

A
B

> The R_f value for a compound changes in _____, so the _____ of spots can also change in _____.

Topic 8 — Chemical Analysis

Paper Chromatography

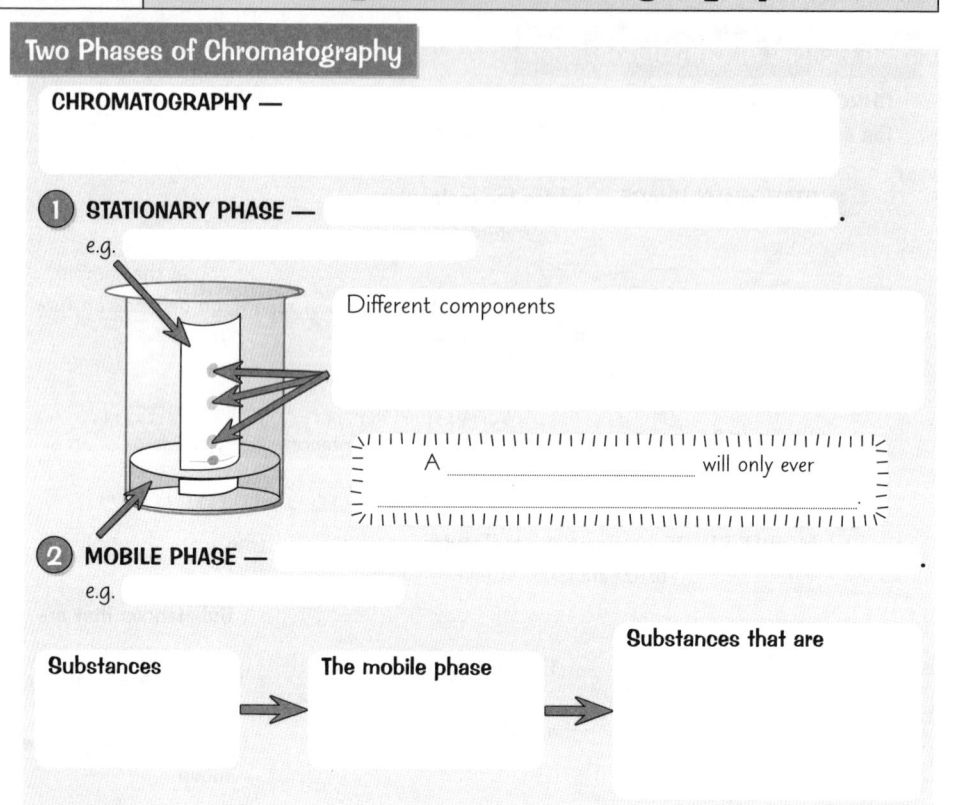

Second Go: ...../...../.....

Two Phases of Chromatography

CHROMATOGRAPHY —

① **STATIONARY PHASE —** _____ .

e.g.

Different components _____

A _____ will only ever _____ .

② **MOBILE PHASE —** _____ .

e.g.

Substances → The mobile phase → Substances that are

R_f Values

R_f VALUE —

$R_f =$

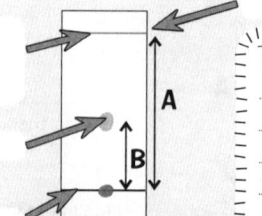

A
B

The R_f value _____ , so the _____ .

Topic 8 — Chemical Analysis

Tests for Ions

First Go: ...../...../.....

Anions and Cations

ANION	An ion with a _____ charge.
CATION	An ion with a _____ charge.

Test for Sulfates

Add _____ hydrochloric acid followed by _____ solution to mystery solution.

If sulfate (_____) ions are present, a _____ will form.

Test for Halides

Add dilute _____ followed by _____ solution to mystery solution.

Chloride (_____) ions give a _____ precipitate. — silver chloride

_____ (Br⁻) ions give a _____ precipitate.

_____ ions give a yellow precipitate.

Test for Carbonates

Add a couple of drops of _____ .

↓

Connect the _____ to a test tube of _____ .

↓

Carbonate ions react to form _____ , which will turn the limewater _____ .

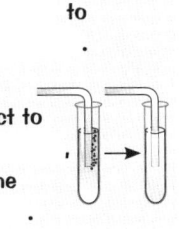

Test for Metal Cations with NaOH

Add a few drops of _____ (NaOH) solution to mystery solution.

Metal Ion	Colour of Precipitate	Ionic Equation
Calcium, Ca^{2+}		$Ca^{2+}_{(aq)}$ + _____ → $Ca(OH)_{2(s)}$
	Blue	_____ + $2OH^-_{(aq)}$ →
Iron(II), Fe^{2+}		
Iron( ),	Brown	_____ + $3OH^-_{(aq)}$ → $Fe(OH)_{3(s)}$
_____ , Al^{3+}	(Redissolves in _____ NaOH to form a colourless solution.)	$Al^{3+}_{(aq)}$ + $3OH^-_{(aq)}$ →
Magnesium,		

Topic 8 — Chemical Analysis

Tests for Ions

Second Go: ..... / ..... / .....

Anions and Cations

ANION	
CATION	

Test for Halides

Add dilute

Test for Sulfates

Add dilute

If sulfate

Test for Carbonates

Add

↓

Connect

↓

Carbonate ions

Test for Metal Cations with NaOH

Add _____ to mystery solution.

Metal Ion	Colour of Precipitate	Ionic Equation
Calcium,		$Ca^{2+}_{(aq)} + 2OH^-_{(aq)} \rightarrow Ca(OH)_{2(s)}$
	Blue	
Iron(II), Fe^{2+}		
	Brown	
		$Al^{3+}_{(aq)} + 3OH^-_{(aq)} \rightarrow$
	White	

Topic 8 — Chemical Analysis

Flame Tests and Spectroscopy

First Go: ..... /..... /.....

Flame Tests for Metal Cations

Lithium ions | _____ ions | Potassium ions | _____ ions | _____ ions
 | Na^+ | | | Cu^{2+}

crimson flame | _____ flame | _____ flame | orange-red flame | _____ flame

Disadvantage of flame tests — if the sample _____ of metal ions, the _____ of some ions may be _____ by _____.

Three Advantages of Instrumental Analysis

INSTRUMENTAL ANALYSIS — using _____ to analyse _____.

1. Sensitive — can detect even _____
2. Fast — tests can be _____
3. _____

Two Uses of Flame Emission Spectroscopy

Flame emission spectroscopy is an example of _____.

Sample heated in _____. analysed in a _____.

A _____ of different _____ of light is produced.

If _____ are present in a sample, the spectrum will be _____.

Line spectra can be used to:

1. Identify ions in _____ — each _____ ion has a _____ line spectrum.
2. Determine the _____ of ions — this can be calculated from the _____ of the lines.

Topic 8 — Chemical Analysis

110

Second Go: ..... / ..... / .....

Flame Tests and Spectroscopy

Flame Tests for Metal Cations

Lithium	Sodium	Potassium	Calcium	Copper

Disadvantage of flame tests —

Three Advantages of Instrumental Analysis

INSTRUMENTAL ANALYSIS —

1. Sensitive —
2. .... — tests can be ....
3.

Two Uses of Flame Emission Spectroscopy

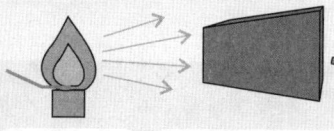

Flame emission spectroscopy ....

Sample   Light   A line spectrum

.... can be used to:

1. Identify
2. Determine

If .... in a sample, ...

Topic 8 — Chemical Analysis

Mixed Practice Quizzes

That's a lot of facts to remember. Luckily for you, there's a handy set of quizzes here to test how much you've remembered from p.103-110.

Quiz 1 — Date: ...... / ...... / ......

1) Give one use of flame emission spectroscopy.
2) How can you test for carbonate ions?
3) What effect do impurities have on the boiling point of a substance?
4) Which gas will relight a glowing splint?
5) True or false? An impure substance will always separate into the same number of spots during chromatography.
6) Give three examples of common formulations.
7) What name is given to a positively charged ion?
8) What is the definition of an R_f value?
9) What colour is the flame when you burn potassium ions?
10) What is the chemical definition of a pure substance?

Total:

Quiz 2 — Date: ...... / ...... / ......

1) What determines the properties of a formulation?
2) Give two advantages of instrumental analysis.
3) What effect does chlorine gas have on damp litmus paper?
4) What name is given to an aqueous solution of calcium hydroxide?
5) Name a substance that can be used as the mobile phase in chromatography.
6) In chromatography, what does the amount of separation of the different components in a sample depend on?
7) What is chromatography?
8) What colour precipitate is formed when NaOH is added to a solution containing Cu^{2+} ions?
9) Which metal ion burns with a crimson flame?
10) What is added to a mystery solution to test for the presence of halides?

Total:

Topic 8 — Chemical Analysis

Mixed Practice Quizzes

Quiz 3   Date: ...... / ...... / ......

1) What is commonly used as the stationary phase in chromatography?
2) True or false? A chemically pure substance melts at a specific temperature.
3) How can a lighted splint be used to identify hydrogen gas?
4) What type of charge does a cation have?
5) What colour is the precipitate formed when NaOH solution is added to a solution containing Fe^{2+} ions?
6) How can the R_f value of a substance in a particular solvent be calculated?
7) Give one example of a method of instrumental analysis.
8) How many spots are formed by a pure substance during chromatography?
9) True or false? In chromatography, substances that are less soluble in the mobile phase travel further through the stationary phase.
10) Describe how you would test for the presence of sulfate ions in a solution.

Total:

Quiz 4   Date: ...... / ...... / ......

1) Give the formula of the brown precipitate formed when sodium hydroxide solution is added to a solution of Fe^{3+} ions.
2) True or false? Medicines are chemical formulations.
3) Give a disadvantage of using a flame test to identify metal ions.
4) Do compounds have the same R_f value in every solvent?
5) What colour is a precipitate of silver bromide?
6) What does the line spectrum for a sample containing multiple ions consist of?
7) Explain how a substance separates out during chromatography.
8) Describe a chemical test that you can use to distinguish between a substance containing Al^{3+} ions and a substance containing Mg^{2+} ions.
9) Which metal ion burns with a yellow flame?
10) What is observed when dilute hydrochloric acid and barium chloride solution are added to a solution containing sulfate ions?

Total:

Topic 8 — Chemical Analysis

Topic 9 — Chemistry of the Atmosphere

The Evolution of the Atmosphere

First Go: ..... / ..... / .....

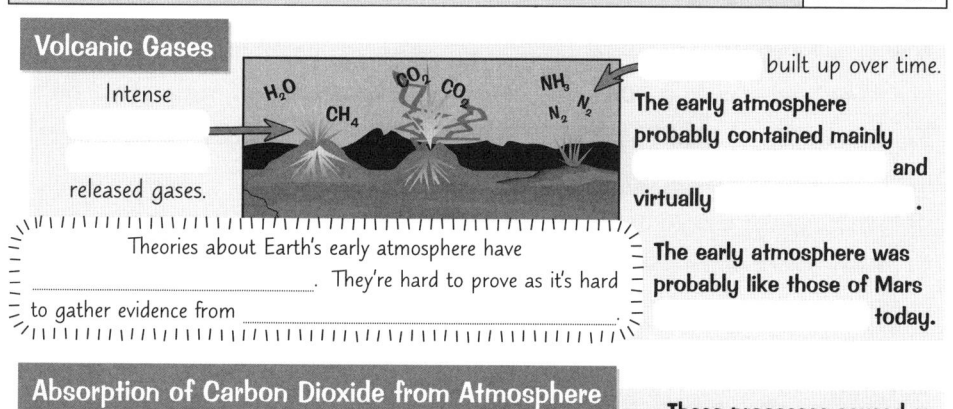

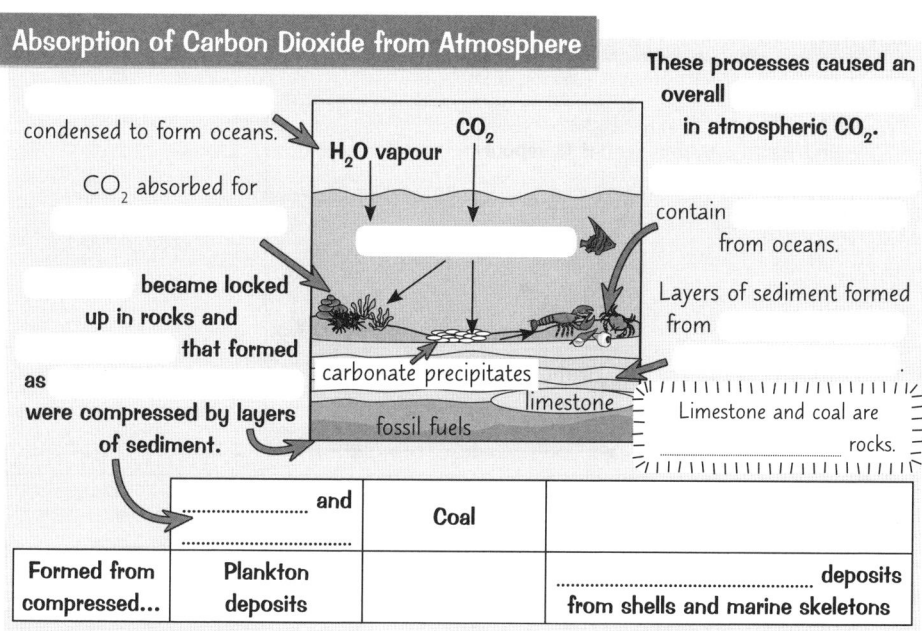

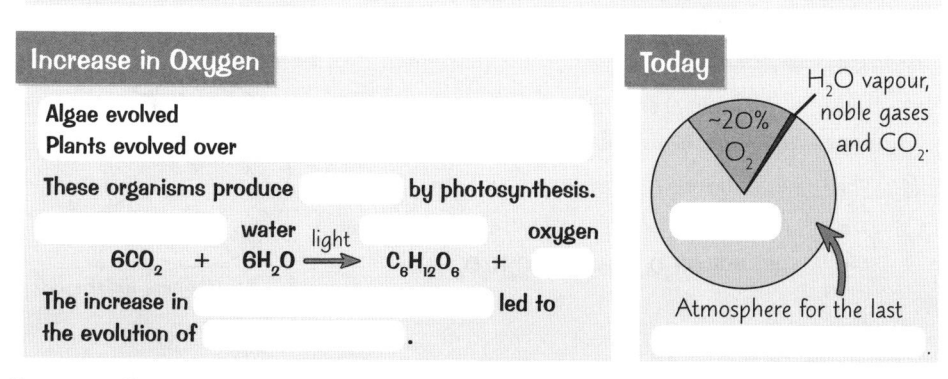

Volcanic Gases

Intense _____ released gases.

_____ built up over time. The early atmosphere probably contained mainly _____ and _____ virtually _____.

Theories about Earth's early atmosphere have _____. They're hard to prove as it's hard to gather evidence from _____.

The early atmosphere was probably like those of Mars _____ today.

Absorption of Carbon Dioxide from Atmosphere

_____ condensed to form oceans.

CO_2 absorbed for _____

_____ became locked up in rocks and _____ that formed as _____ were compressed by layers of sediment.

carbonate precipitates
limestone
fossil fuels

These processes caused an overall _____ in atmospheric CO_2.

_____ contain _____ from oceans.

Layers of sediment formed from _____.

Limestone and coal are _____ rocks.

	_____ and _____	Coal	
Formed from compressed...	Plankton deposits		_____ deposits from shells and marine skeletons

Increase in Oxygen

Algae evolved _____
Plants evolved over _____

These organisms produce _____ by photosynthesis.

$$6CO_2 + 6H_2O \xrightarrow{light} C_6H_{12}O_6 + \text{oxygen}$$
(water)

The increase in _____ led to the evolution of _____.

Today

~20% O_2

H_2O vapour, noble gases and CO_2.

_____

Atmosphere for the last _____

Topic 9 — Chemistry of the Atmosphere

The Evolution of the Atmosphere

Second Go: ..... / ..... / .....

Volcanic Gases

H_2O, CH_4, CO_2, CO_2, NH_3, N_2, N_2

.... built up over time.

Theories about Earth's early atmosphere have .... They're hard to prove as it's hard to ....

Absorption of Carbon Dioxide from Atmosphere

These processes caused ....

condensed to form oceans.

H_2O vapour

.... contain .... from oceans.

carbonate precipitates

Limestone and coal are ....

	Coal	
Formed from compressed...		.... deposits from ....

Increase in Oxygen

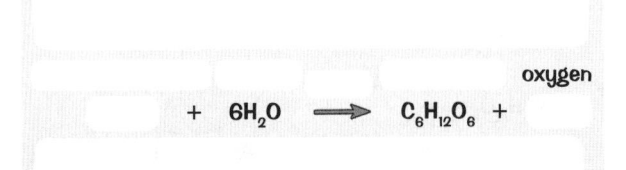

.... + $6H_2O \longrightarrow C_6H_{12}O_6$ + oxygen

Today

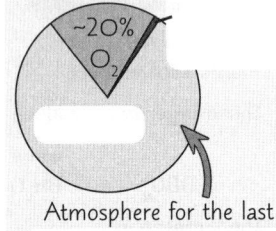

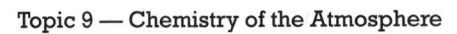

~20% O_2

....

Atmosphere for the last ....

Topic 9 — Chemistry of the Atmosphere

Greenhouse Gases & Climate Change

First Go: ...../...../.....

The Greenhouse Effect

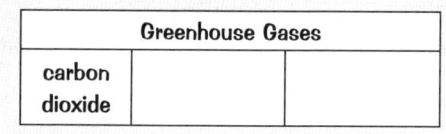

Greenhouse Gases		
carbon dioxide		

GREENHOUSE EFFECT — when greenhouse gases in the .... absorb .... and re-radiate it in all directions, including back towards Earth, helping to keep the ....

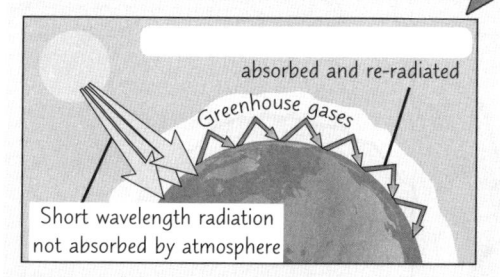

absorbed and re-radiated
Greenhouse gases
Short wavelength radiation not absorbed by atmosphere

Human Activities

Deforestation means less .... is removed by ....

.... fossil fuels releases ....

Causes of increased .... and ....

Farm animals produce ....

Decomposition of landfill and agricultural waste releases .... and ....

Climate Change Evidence

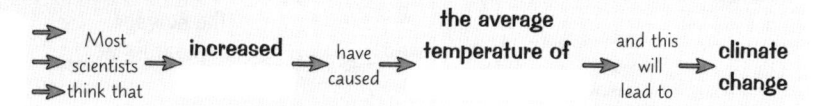

→ Most
→ scientists → increased .... → have caused → the average temperature of .... → and this will lead to → climate change

.... is very complex and hard to model. This leads to oversimplified .... in the media where stories are biased or ....

Four Possible Consequences of Climate Change

1. Flooding and erosion in .... due to the melting of the .... causing sea levels to rise.

2. More frequent and severe ....

3. .... in certain areas if temperature and ....

4. Changes in the .... of some wild species if ....

Topic 9 — Chemistry of the Atmosphere

Second Go: ..... / ..... / .....

Greenhouse Gases & Climate Change

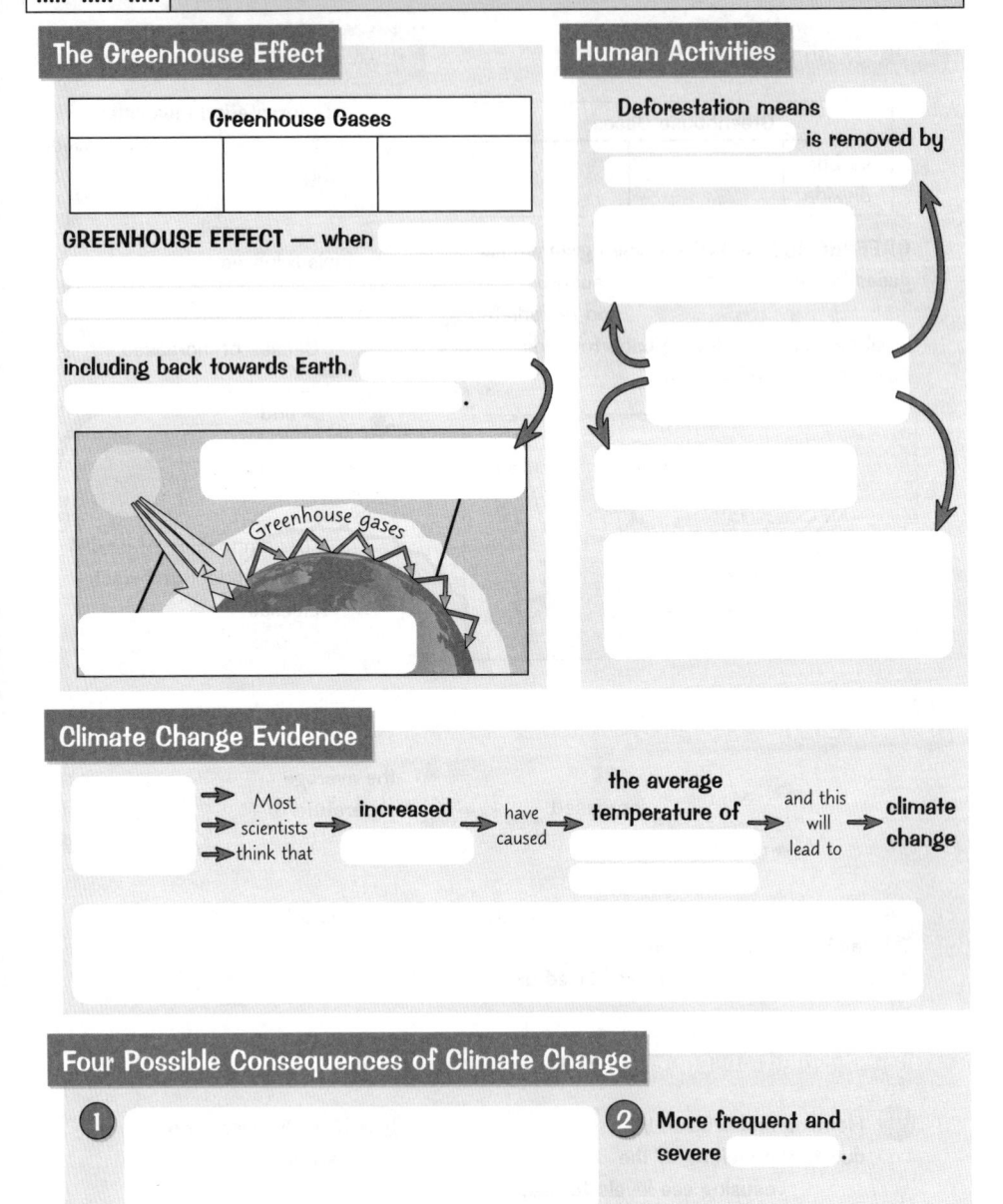

The Greenhouse Effect

	Greenhouse Gases	

GREENHOUSE EFFECT — when _____
_____
_____

including back towards Earth, _____.

Human Activities

Deforestation means _____
_____ is removed by
_____

_____

_____

_____

_____

Climate Change Evidence

→ Most scientists → think that → _____ → increased → have caused → the average temperature of → _____ → and this will lead to → climate change

Four Possible Consequences of Climate Change

1) _____

2) More frequent and severe _____.

3) _____ in certain areas if temperature and _____.

4) Changes in the _____ of some wild species if _____.

Topic 9 — Chemistry of the Atmosphere

Carbon Footprints and Air Pollution

First Go: ..... / ..... / .....

Carbon Footprints

CARBON FOOTPRINT — how much _____ and other greenhouse gases are released over _____ — e.g. _____.

- _____ emissions reduces the carbon footprint.
- Actions to _____ may be limited _____ are unwilling or unable to make _____.

Air Pollution

Fossil fuels contain _____ and sometimes _____.

_____ releases _____ which pollute the air.

doesn't have any colour or smell, so it's hard to _____.

Pollutant	Formation	Effects
....	carbon particulates, water vapour, ...	Stops blood from transporting .... around the body — this can cause .... or ....
carbon particulates (...........)	.... of fossil fuels (e.g. coal).	.... problems Global ....
sulfur dioxide	.... of .... in fossil fuels during combustion.	NO_x → SO_2 → damage to ...., statues and ....
oxides of	Reaction between .... and .... in the air caused by the ...., e.g. in car engines.	.... problems

Topic 9 — Chemistry of the Atmosphere

Second Go:
..... / ..... / .....

Carbon Footprints and Air Pollution

Carbon Footprints

CARBON FOOTPRINT —

- Reducing

•

Air Pollution

Fossil fuels contain .... and sometimes ....

.... doesn't have .... , so it's hard to ....

Pollutant	....	Effects
	water vapour .... of fossil fuels (e.g. coal).	Stops .... around the body — this can cause .... , ... or ....
	Reaction between .... and .... in the air caused by the	NO$_x$ SO$_2$ ....

Topic 9 — Chemistry of the Atmosphere

Mixed Practice Quizzes

A lot to learn there, but p.113-118 will help you understand how Earth's atmosphere has changed over billions of years, as well as helping you to answer these quizzes.

Quiz 1 — Date: ...... / ...... / ......

1) Give one human activity that contributes to increased levels of methane in the atmosphere.
2) What are crude oil and natural gas formed from?
3) Roughly what percentage of the atmosphere today is nitrogen?
4) Which pollutants can react with water in clouds to form acid rain?
5) What is the definition of a carbon footprint?
6) Why is it hard to find evidence about what Earth's early atmosphere was like?
7) Give the balanced symbol equation for photosynthesis.
8) How did the oceans form from the early atmosphere?
9) True or false? The Earth's atmosphere absorbs more long wavelength radiation than short wavelength radiation.
10) Why is it difficult to detect carbon monoxide?

Total:

Quiz 2 — Date: ...... / ...... / ......

1) Give two of the problems caused by carbon particulates in the air.
2) Name three greenhouse gases.
3) How do scientists think that gases were released into the early atmosphere?
4) What are the two products of photosynthesis?
5) How did the formation of oceans lead to a decrease in the amount of carbon dioxide in the atmosphere?
6) Describe one possible negative effect of climate change.
7) Roughly how many years ago did algae evolve?
8) How is sulfur dioxide produced from fossil fuels?
9) What type of rock are coal and limestone?
10) What change in the Earth's early atmosphere enabled animals to evolve?

Total:

Topic 9 — Chemistry of the Atmosphere

Mixed Practice Quizzes

Quiz 3   Date: ...... / ...... / ......

1) Which fossil fuel is formed from compressed plant deposits?
2) How do greenhouse gases in the atmosphere keep the Earth warm?
3) Most scientists believe that increased levels of carbon dioxide will lead to climate change. What is this belief based on?
4) How can a carbon footprint be reduced?
5) How is nitrogen thought to have built up in Earth's early atmosphere?
6) Give one problem associated with increased carbon monoxide in the air.
7) Roughly what percentage of Earth's atmosphere today is oxygen?
8) True or false? Fossil fuel formation resulted in an increase in atmospheric carbon dioxide.
9) Which atmospheric gas is absorbed by plants and algae for photosynthesis?
10) What were the layers of sediment on the seabed formed from?

Total:

Quiz 4   Date: ...... / ...... / ......

1) Give two problems caused by sulfur dioxide pollution.
2) How can burning fuel lead to the production of oxides of nitrogen?
3) Which two planets have atmospheres thought to be similar to that of the early Earth?
4) Name one gas that makes up a small proportion of Earth's current atmosphere today.
5) How were limestone deposits formed?
6) True or false? One theory suggests that the Earth's early atmosphere contained mainly carbon dioxide.
7) Name two pollutants produced by the incomplete combustion of a fuel.
8) Give one problem caused by acid rain.
9) Give one reason why media stories on climate change are often biased or missing information.
10) Name one element which is often found as an impurity in fossil fuels.

Total:

Topic 9 — Chemistry of the Atmosphere

Topic 10 — Using Resources

Materials

First Go: ..../..../....

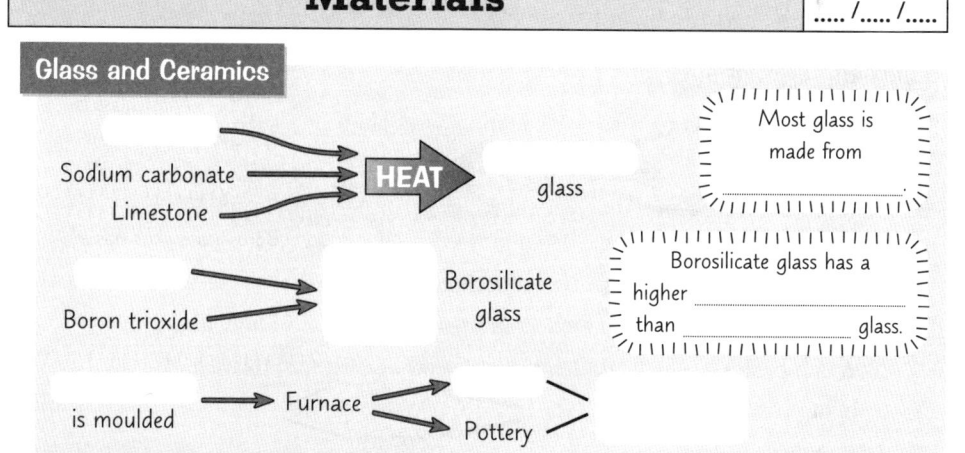

Glass and Ceramics

Sodium carbonate ⟶ HEAT ⟶ _____ glass
Limestone ⟶

Most glass is made from _____.

_____ ⟶ _____ ⟶ Borosilicate glass
Boron trioxide ⟶

Borosilicate glass has a higher _____ than _____ glass.

_____ is moulded ⟶ Furnace ⟶ Pottery ⟶ _____

Four Examples of Composites

COMPOSITES — made up of a _____ surrounding reinforcement fibres or _____.

1. _____ — used for speedboats
2. _____ — used to make racing cars
3. Concrete — a building material
4. Wood — _____

Polymers

Polymers have _____ depending on _____ and _____.

Polymer	How It's Made	Properties
Low density poly(ethene)	Ethene, ..., high pressure	Flexible
	Ethene, lower temperature and pressure, ...	

Polymer properties also depend on how their chains are bonded to each other.

Polymer	.... Bonds	Properties
	Weak forces between	Can be ....
Thermosetting polymers	.... form .... between polymer chains	................, hard, ..., don't melt

Second Go: ...../...../.....

Materials

Glass and Ceramics

[diagram: two inputs → HEAT → glass]

Most glass is made from ....

[diagram: inputs → Borosilicate glass]

Borosilicate glass has a ....

[diagram: input → process → Pottery →]

Four Examples of Composites

COMPOSITES —

1.
2.
3.
4.

Polymers

Polymers have

Polymer	How It's Made	Properties
Low density poly(ethene)		

Polymer .... also depend on how their chains are bonded to each other.

Polymer	.... Bonds	Properties
	.... form .... between	..........,'..........,' ...., don't melt

Topic 10 — Using Resources

Metals and Corrosion

First Go: ..../..../....

Seven Examples of Alloys

1. Gold + ⟶ **GOLD ALLOYS**

2. Copper + Zinc ⟶ Taps

   24 carat gold = 100% gold
   18 carat gold = 75% gold

3. ___ + Tin ⟶ **BRONZE** Medals

4. Iron + Carbon ⟶ Cars

5. Iron + Carbon ⟶ **HIGH CARBON STEEL** (strong but brittle) Bridges

6. Iron + ___ ⟶ **STAINLESS STEEL** (hard, resistant to corrosion) Cutlery

7. Aluminium + Various Other Metals ⟶ **ALUMINIUM ALLOYS** (low density)

Corrosion and Rusting

CORROSION — where ___ with substances in their environment and are ___.

RUSTING — corrosion of iron by ___.

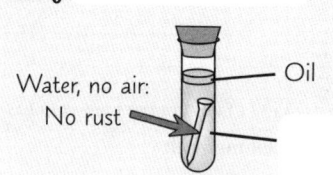

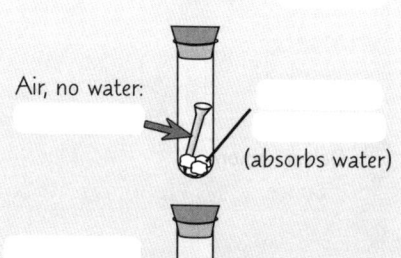

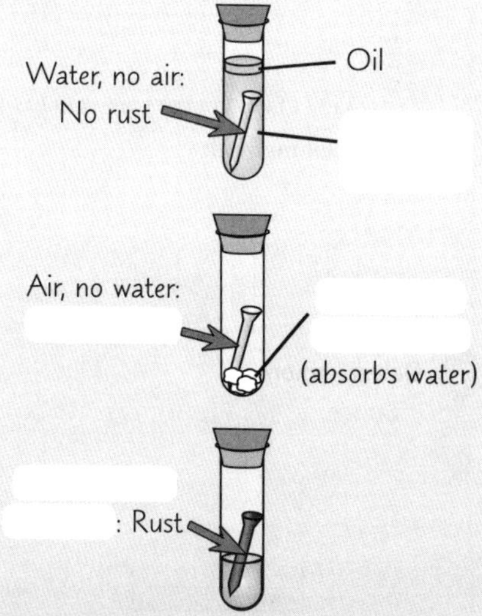

Water, no air: No rust — Oil

Air, no water: ___ (absorbs water)

___ : Rust

Three Ways to Prevent Rusting

1. **Barrier methods:** Painting, greasing and ___ iron to keep out ___ and ___.

   Aluminium has an ___ which protects against ___.

2. **Sacrificial method:** Attaching a ___ to iron.

3. **Galvanisation:** Both a ___. Iron is coated with a layer of more reactive ___.

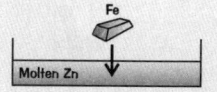

Fe
Molten Zn

Topic 10 — Using Resources

Second Go: ...../...../.....

Metals and Corrosion

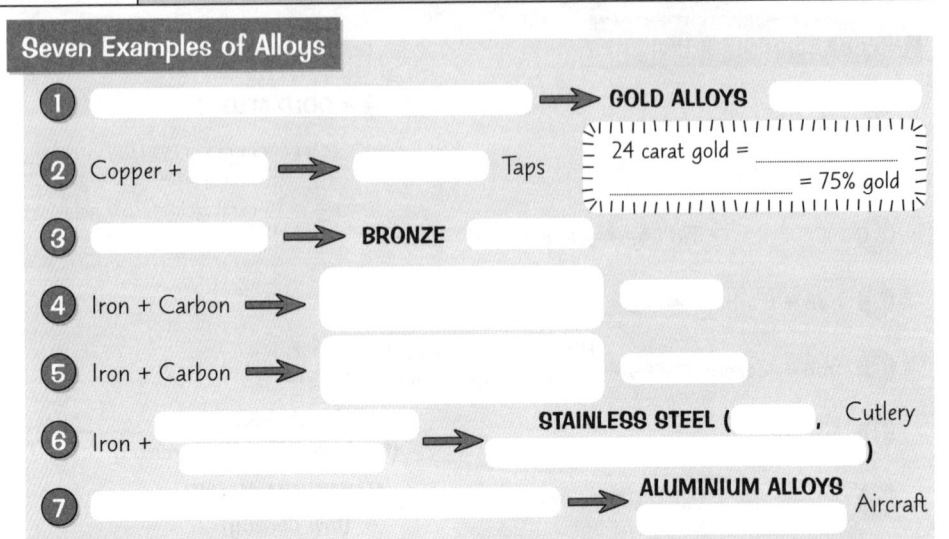

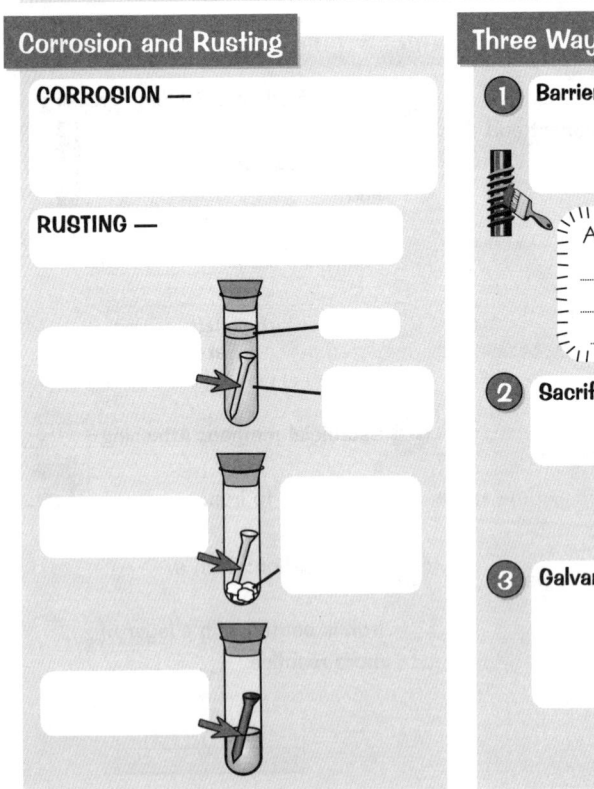

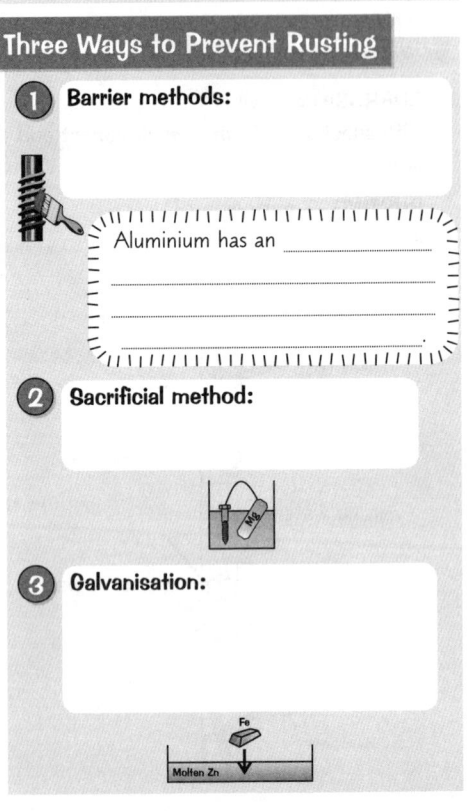

Seven Examples of Alloys

1. _____ → **GOLD ALLOYS** _____
   - 24 carat gold = _____
   - _____ = 75% gold
2. Copper + _____ → _____ Taps
3. _____ → **BRONZE** _____
4. Iron + Carbon → _____ _____
5. Iron + Carbon → _____
6. Iron + _____ → **STAINLESS STEEL** (_____, Cutlery _____)
7. _____ → **ALUMINIUM ALLOYS** Aircraft _____

Corrosion and Rusting

CORROSION — _____

RUSTING — _____

Three Ways to Prevent Rusting

1. **Barrier methods:** _____

   Aluminium has an _____

2. **Sacrificial method:** _____

3. **Galvanisation:** _____

Topic 10 — Using Resources

Resources & Life Cycle Assessments

First Go: ..... / ..... / .....

Resources

Humans use _____ for a variety of different purposes:

Clothing   Shelter   Fuel for transport

We can use _____ products in place of certain natural resources, e.g. rubber can be replaced by _____.

Some natural resources are FINITE — _____.

Nuclear fuel   _____   Coal

_____ are processed to provide materials and energy.

RENEWABLE RESOURCES — resources that reform at a _____, e.g. timber.

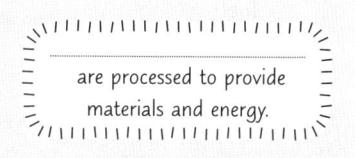

Life Cycle Assessments

LIFE CYCLE ASSESSMENT (LCA) — an assessment of the _____ of a product over each stage of its life.

Life Cycle Assessment Stage	Plastic Bag	Paper Bag
		Timber
Manufacturing and Packaging	Key compounds extracted by .... Waste has other uses.	Takes a lot of energy to pulp timber and creates lots of waste
	Reusable	
Product	Recyclable, ...	.... and recyclable

- Some factors _____ are easily quantified.
- Some factors _____ are hard to measure or depend on a person's opinion. This can make life cycle assessments biased.
- **SELECTIVE LCA** — LCA where _____ has been removed to make _____ than it really is.

Topic 10 — Using Resources

Resources & Life Cycle Assessments

Second Go: ..... / ..... / .....

Resources

Humans use _____ :

_____   Clothing   Shelter   Fuel for _____   _____

We can use _____ in place of certain _____, e.g. _____ can be replaced by _____.

Some natural resources are FINITE — _____.

_____ fuel _____
RENEWABLE RESOURCES — _____ _____ are processed to provide _____.

Life Cycle Assessments

LIFE CYCLE ASSESSMENT (LCA) — _____

Life Cycle Assessment Stage	Plastic Bag	Paper Bag
Raw Materials		
	Reusable	
Product Disposal		

- Some factors _____

- Some factors _____ are hard to measure or depend on a person's opinion. This can make _____.

- **SELECTIVE LCA** — _____

Topic 10 — Using Resources

Reuse and Recycling

First Go: ..... / ..... / .....

Improving Sustainability

Mining for raw materials is bad for the _____.

SUSTAINABLE DEVELOPMENT — meeting the needs of present society while not damaging the lives of _____.

Three ways to improve sustainability:
1. _____ the amount of raw materials used as well as the _____.
2. Reusing products instead of _____ reduces the amount of _____ we need to extract, _____ involved in their extraction.
3. _____ products that can't be _____.

Copper Ores

Copper ore is a _____ that is becoming scarce.
We can improve sustainability by _____.

Phytomining — containing copper → copper → harvested plants are _____ — ash contains copper

Bioleaching — bacteria → bacteria convert copper compounds → solution → Pure copper extracted → reaction with _____

Recycling Metals

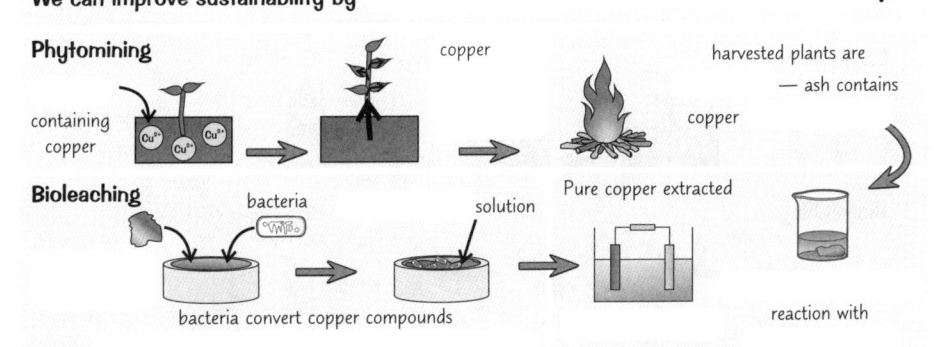

Recycling metals helps to save on the _____ required to mine and _____.

_____ → Melted down → _____ into new products

Amount of _____ required for recyclable metals depends on the _____ and _____.

Both _____ and _____ can be added to iron in a _____ together to reduce the amount of _____ required.

Recycling Glass

Waste glass
↓
Separated by colour and _____
↓
_____
↓
Reshaped

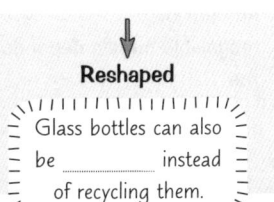

Glass bottles can also be _____ instead of recycling them.

Topic 10 — Using Resources

Reuse and Recycling

Second Go: ...../...../......

Improving Sustainability

Mining for raw materials is bad for the _____.

_____ — meeting the needs of present society _____.

Three ways to improve sustainability:

1. Reducing
2. Reusing
3. _____ products that can't be _____

_____ reduces the amount of _____ as well as the _____.

Copper Ores

Copper ore ....
....
....

Phytomining

copper _____

_____ — ash contains copper _____

Bioleaching

_____ _____

Pure copper extracted

_____

Recycling Metals

Recycling metals _____

_____ → Melted down → _____

Amount of _____ required for recyclable metals depends on the _____.

Both _____ and _____ can be added to _____
....
....

Recycling Glass

Waste glass
↓
_____
↓
_____

Glass bottles can also be _____ instead of recycling them.

Topic 10 — Using Resources

Mixed Practice Quizzes

There was a lot to go over on p.121-128, but you've made it through. Use these quizzes to check how much has sunk in before carrying on to the second half.

Quiz 1   Date: ...... / ...... / ......

1) Which two elements are contained in bronze?
2) What is meant by a 'renewable resource'?
3) Give one benefit of borosilicate glass over soda-lime glass.
4) Which type of poly(ethene) is produced with a catalyst?
5) What two things does the amount of separation required for recycling metals depend on?
6) Which method of copper extraction uses bacteria to convert copper compounds in the ore to soluble copper compounds?
7) 24 carat gold contains what percentage of gold?
8) What two conditions are required for iron to rust?
9) What do composites consist of?
10) Give one use of gold alloys.

Total:

Quiz 2   Date: ...... / ...... / ......

1) What property of aluminium alloys makes them useful in the production of aircraft?
2) Give an example of a natural resource that can be replaced by a man-made product.
3) What is carried out to identify the environmental impact of a new product?
4) Name a composite that is commonly used to make speedboats.
5) What are the steps involved in recycling glass?
6) What holds the polymer chains in a thermosoftening polymer together?
7) Which rust prevention method is both a barrier and a sacrificial method?
8) What is corrosion?
9) Give one example of a finite resource.
10) State a benefit of recycling metals.

Total:

Topic 10 — Using Resources

Mixed Practice Quizzes

Quiz 3 Date: ...... / ...... / ......

1) What are two properties of stainless steel?
2) Will iron rust if it is placed in a test tube with a large enough quantity of calcium chloride?
3) Why is aluminium naturally resistant to corrosion?
4) What are the three components of soda-lime glass?
5) Give an example of a natural composite.
6) Give two properties of thermosetting polymers.
7) Name an alloy used to build bridges.
8) Name two elements which can be added to gold to produce gold alloys.
9) What alloy is made up of copper and tin?
10) What is meant by a selective LCA?

Total:

Quiz 4 Date: ...... / ...... / ......

1) State three purposes which humans use natural resources for.
2) Give two examples of clay ceramics.
3) Which type of poly(ethene) is produced at high pressure?
4) What metal is used to galvanise iron?
5) What is the purpose of sustainable development?
6) Why might two LCAs on the same product be different?
7) Give one way that pure copper can be extracted from the compounds produced by phytomining or bioleaching.
8) Give two methods of adding a protective barrier to a metal.
9) Why is low carbon steel used to produce cars?
10) Give the four stages of a product's life that are considered in a life cycle assessment.

Total:

Topic 10 — Using Resources

Treating Water

First Go:
...../...../.....

Potable Water

POTABLE WATER —

Potable water is not _____.
It can contain low levels of _____ and _____.

Type of Water	Source	
Ground water		Must be _____ and sterilised
Salt water	Sea water	Must be _____
	Sewage treatment and agricultural systems	Requires a lot of treatment

Treating Ground Water

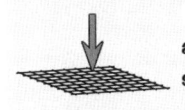

_____ — to remove any large debris such as _____

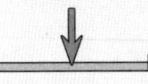

filtration — to remove any smaller _____

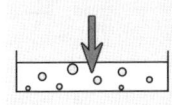

Sterilisation — to kill off any harmful _____ using _____, ozone or _____

This is how rainwater collected in the _____, _____ and _____ is treated in the UK.

Two Methods of Desalination

Desalination is carried out in _____ to make sea water _____.

1. DISTILLATION — _____ the water to separate it from _____.

2. _____ — passing the water through a _____ that only allows _____ through.

These methods use _____.

Treating Waste Water

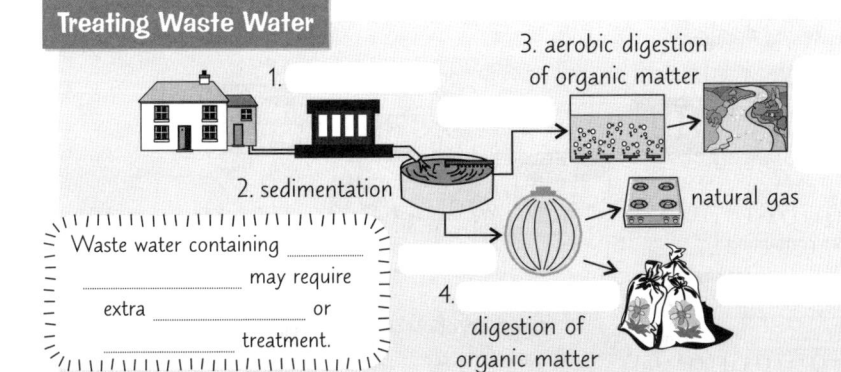

1. _____
2. sedimentation
3. aerobic digestion of organic matter
4. _____ digestion of organic matter

natural gas

Waste water containing _____ may require extra _____ or _____ treatment.

Topic 10 — Using Resources

Treating Water

Second Go: ..... / ..... / .....

Potable Water

POTABLE WATER —

Potable water is .... It can contain low levels of .... and ....

Type of Water	Source	
Ground water		
Salt water		

Treating Ground Water

.... — to remove ....

Sterilisation — ....

This is how rainwater collected in the ...., ... and .... is treated in the UK.

Two Methods of Desalination

Desalination ....

1. **DISTILLATION** — ....

2. .... — passing the water ....

These methods use ....

Treating Waste Water

3. ....

1. ....

2. ....

organic matter

4. digestion of organic matter

Waste water containing .... may require extra .... or .... treatment.

Topic 10 — Using Resources

The Haber Process

First Go: ..... / ..... / .....

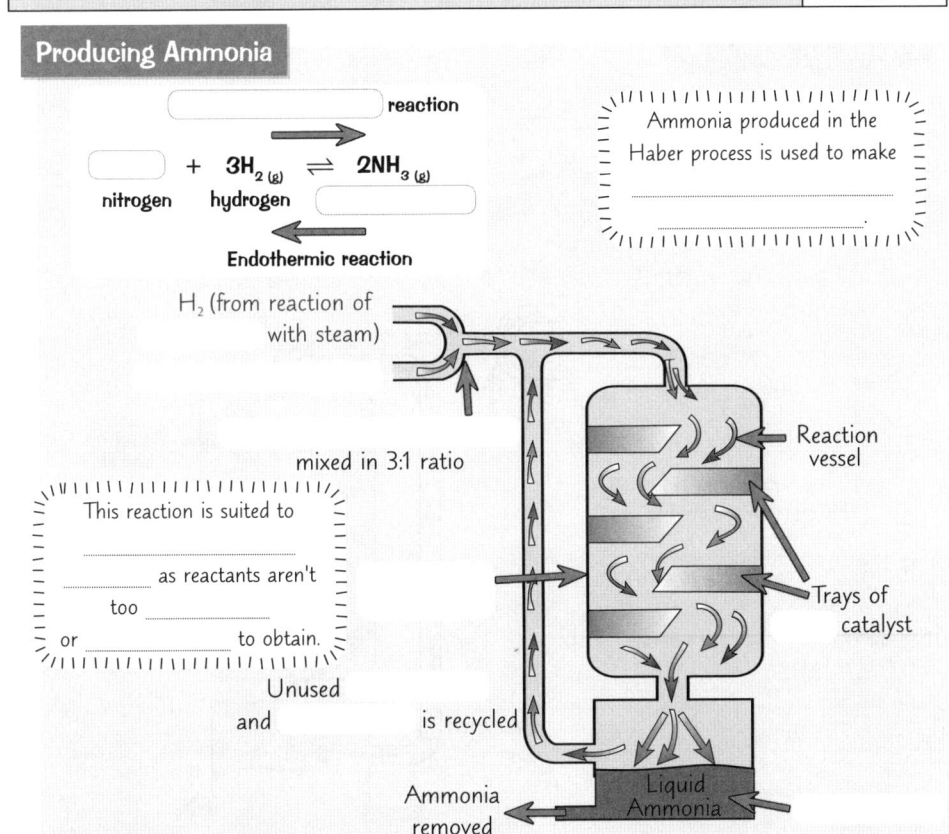

Producing Ammonia

[_____] reaction

[___] + 3H$_{2(g)}$ ⇌ 2NH$_{3(g)}$ [___]
nitrogen   hydrogen

Endothermic reaction

Ammonia produced in the Haber process is used to make _____.

H$_2$ (from reaction of _____ with steam)

mixed in 3:1 ratio

This reaction is suited to _____ as reactants aren't too _____ or _____ to obtain.

Reaction vessel

Trays of catalyst

Unused _____ and _____ is recycled

Ammonia removed

Liquid Ammonia

Reaction Conditions

	Higher Temperature	Lower Temperature	Higher Pressure	
Yield			Higher	Lower
Rate	Faster	Slower		Slower

Higher temperatures would make the reaction _____, but also favour the _____, lowering the yield.

The reaction temperature of 450 °C is a compromise between a _____ and a higher yield.

Pressure is kept _____ without becoming _____.

Topic 10 — Using Resources

The Haber Process

Second Go: ...../...../.....

Producing Ammonia

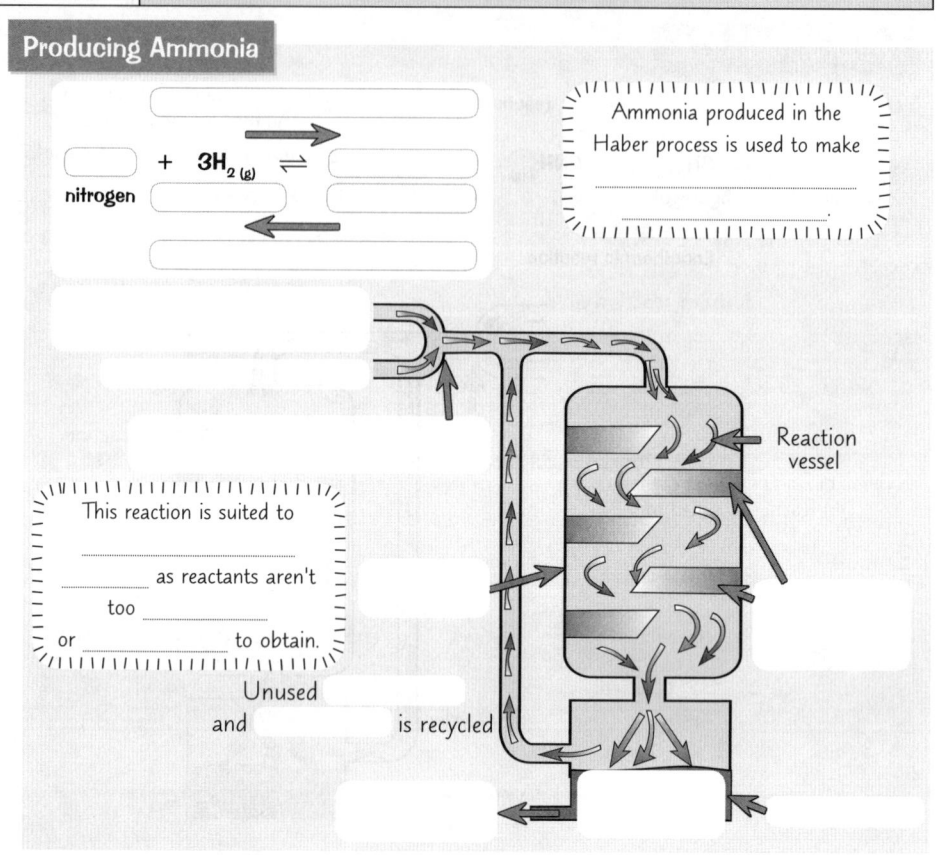

nitrogen + $3H_{2(g)}$ ⇌

Ammonia produced in the Haber process is used to make ....

This reaction is suited to .... as reactants aren't too .... or .... to obtain.

Unused .... and .... is recycled

Reaction vessel

Reaction Conditions

	.... Temperature		Higher	
			Higher	
		Slower		

.... would make ...., but also favour the ....

Pressure .... without becoming ....

Topic 10 — Using Resources

NPK Fertilisers

First Go: ...../...../.....

Key Elements

Three key elements in fertilisers:

Plants need these elements to ....
and ....

NPK FERTILISERS — formulations of salts containing the .... to help plants grow.

Production of Ammonium Nitrate

.... is used to produce ....

Ammonia is then .... to make ammonium nitrate:

$NH_{3(aq)}$ + $HNO_{3(aq)}$ → ammonium nitrate

ammonia

Ammonium nitrate is a good .... because it contains ....

	Production	Result
In Industry	In .... at .... concentration	.... reaction, producing a .... ammonium nitrate product
	.... and .... at .... concentrations	.... reaction, producing .... ammonium nitrate ....

Sources of Potassium and Phosphorus

.... and .... are mined and used as a source of ....

Phosphate rock can also be mined, but must be .... to produce ....

Phosphate rock + ...	Products
	.... and calcium nitrate
	.... and calcium phosphate
Phosphoric acid	

Topic 10 — Using Resources

Second Go: ..... /..... /.....

NPK Fertilisers

Key Elements

Three key elements in fertilisers:

_____.

_____ need these elements to _____.

NPK FERTILISERS —

Production of Ammonium Nitrate

_____ is used to produce _____.

Ammonia is then _____ to make → _____ + _____ → _____

ammonium nitrate:

> Ammonium nitrate is a good _____ because _____.

	Production	Result
In Industry		
In Laboratory		

Sources of Potassium and Phosphorus

_____
and used as _____.
Phosphate rock can also be _____, but must be _____.

Phosphate rock + ...	Products
	.... and ....
	.... and ....

Topic 10 — Using Resources

Mixed Practice Quizzes

Congratulations, you've made it all the way to the end of Topic 10.
Now collect your prize — four perfectly constructed quizzes all about p.131-136.

Quiz 1   Date: ...... / ...... / ......

1) What are the reactants in the Haber process?
2) How are small solids removed from ground water?
3) What is meant by 'potable water'?
4) What is produced by the reaction of phosphate rock with nitric acid?
5) Why do high temperatures reduce the yield of the Haber process?
6) What are the three key elements in NPK fertilisers?
7) How does increasing the pressure affect the yield of the Haber process?
8) What is the ammonia produced by the Haber process used for?
9) What happens to the effluent from the treatment of waste water before it is released to the environment?
10) Give a problem associated with desalinating water.

Total:

Quiz 2   Date: ...... / ...... / ......

1) State the temperature and pressure used in the Haber process.
2) Is potable water chemically pure?
3) Describe the purpose of the sterilisation stage of ground water treatment.
4) Is it easiest to obtain potable water from ground water, waste water or salt water?
5) Why is a low temperature not used in the Haber process in order to maximise yield?
6) Why is an extremely high pressure not used in the Haber process?
7) True or false? Phosphate rock can be used as a fertiliser immediately after mining it.
8) Give two key sources of potassium for use in fertilisers.
9) Which method of desalination involves boiling the water?
10) Give an example of a salt that is made using ammonia.

Total:

Topic 10 — Using Resources

Mixed Practice Quizzes

Quiz 3   Date: ...... / ...... / ......

1) What is used as the catalyst in the Haber process?
2) What are the two products of the sedimentation of waste water?
3) Is the forward reaction in the Haber process exothermic or endothermic?
4) What is the source of the fresh water that collects in the ground and lakes and rivers?
5) What is produced when phosphate rock reacts with sulfuric acid?
6) What is the purpose of NPK fertilisers?
7) Is the ammonia produced in the Haber process removed as a gas or a liquid?
8) Describe what happens in the reverse osmosis of sea water.
9) What happens to unreacted hydrogen and nitrogen in the Haber process?
10) True or false? Phosphate rock can be used to produce calcium phosphate.

Total:

Quiz 4   Date: ...... / ...... / ......

1) What fertilisers are formulations of salts containing nitrogen, potassium and phosphorus?
2) How does reducing the temperature affect the rate of the Haber process?
3) What can be used to kill off harmful microbes during the sterilisation stage of ground water treatment?
4) How are potassium chloride and potassium sulfate obtained?
5) What is the first stage of waste water treatment?
6) Which reaction produces the hydrogen used in the Haber process?
7) What is the chemical formula of ammonia?
8) What is produced when phosphate rock reacts with phosphoric acid?
9) Where is the nitrogen used in the Haber process obtained from?
10) True or false? In the UK, potable water is mainly obtained by desalination of salt water.

Total:

Topic 10 — Using Resources

Required Practicals

Required Practicals 1

First Go: ..... /..... /.....

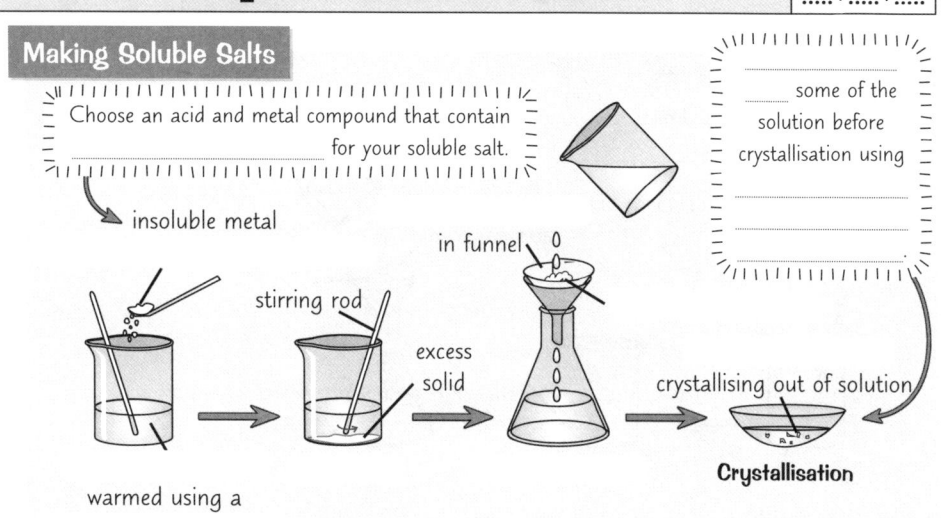

Making Soluble Salts

Choose an acid and metal compound that contain .... for your soluble salt.

.... some of the solution before crystallisation using ....

insoluble metal

stirring rod

in funnel

excess solid

crystallising out of solution

Crystallisation

warmed using a ....

After crystallising the soluble salt, leave it .... to dry.

Titrations

containing a strong acid of ....

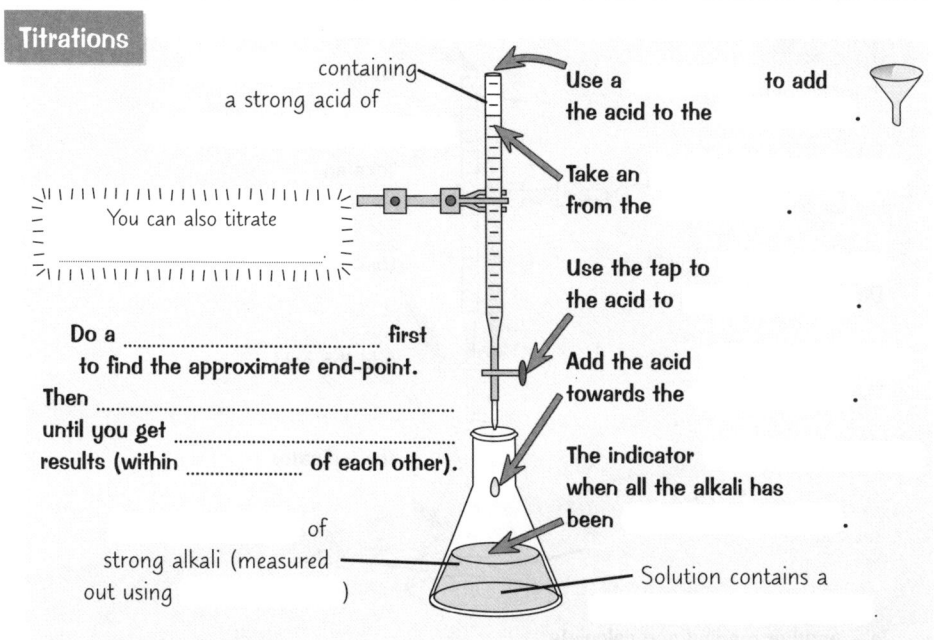

Use a .... to add the acid to the ....

You can also titrate ....

Take an .... from the ....

Use the tap to .... the acid to ....

Do a .... first to find the approximate end-point.
Then ....
until you get .... results (within .... of each other).

Add the acid .... towards the ....

The indicator .... when all the alkali has been ....

.... of strong alkali (measured out using ....)

Solution contains a ....

Take another reading and .... at the end-point: difference between the two readings.

Then you can use your data to calculate ....

Required Practicals

Required Practicals 1

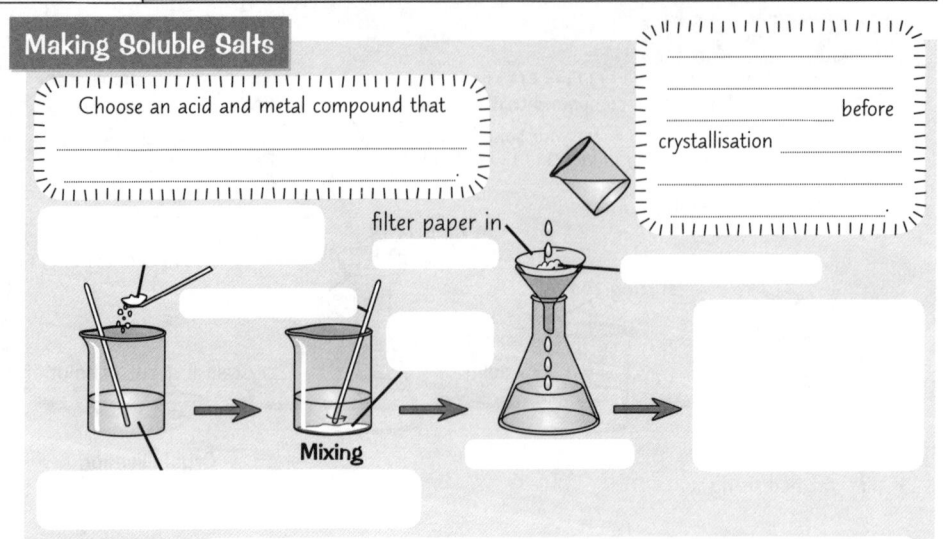

Second Go: ...../...../.....

Making Soluble Salts

Choose an acid and metal compound that ....

.... before crystallisation ....

filter paper in

Mixing

After crystallising ....

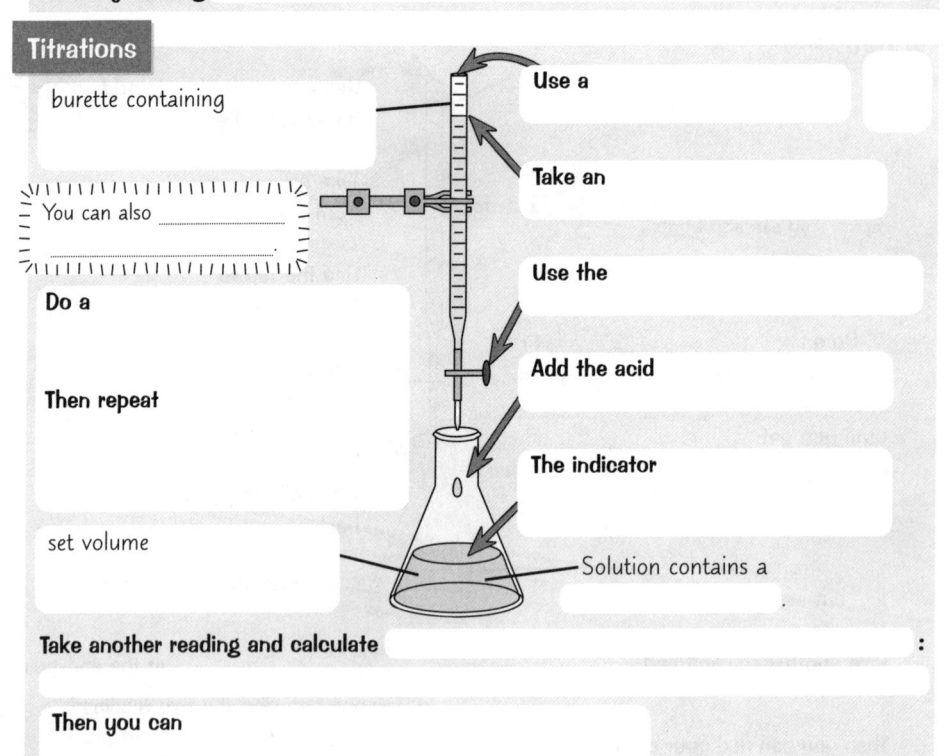

Titrations

burette containing ....

You can also ....

Do a

Then repeat

set volume

Use a

Take an

Use the

Add the acid

The indicator

Solution contains a ....

Take another reading and calculate ....:

Then you can

Required Practicals

Required Practicals 2

First Go:
..... /..... /.....

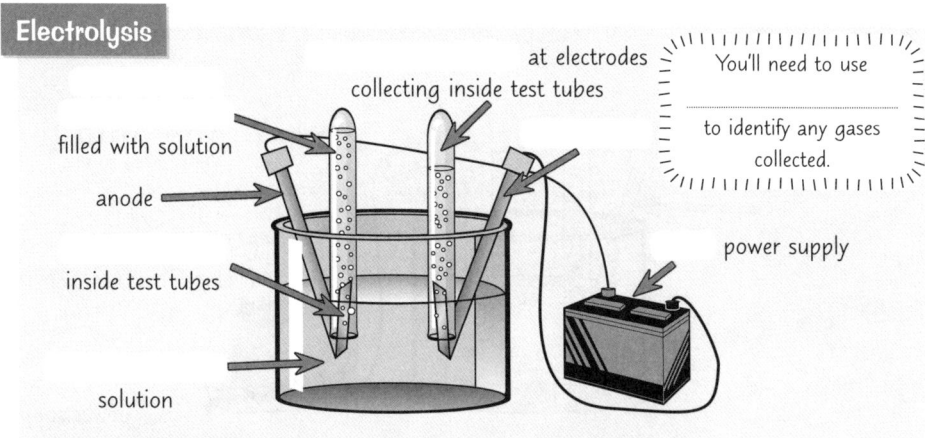

Electrolysis

at electrodes
collecting inside test tubes

filled with solution
anode
inside test tubes
solution

You'll need to use .... to identify any gases collected.

power supply

Product at Anode ( )	Product at ( )
Either bubbles of .... gas or	Either a coating of .... or bubbles of ....

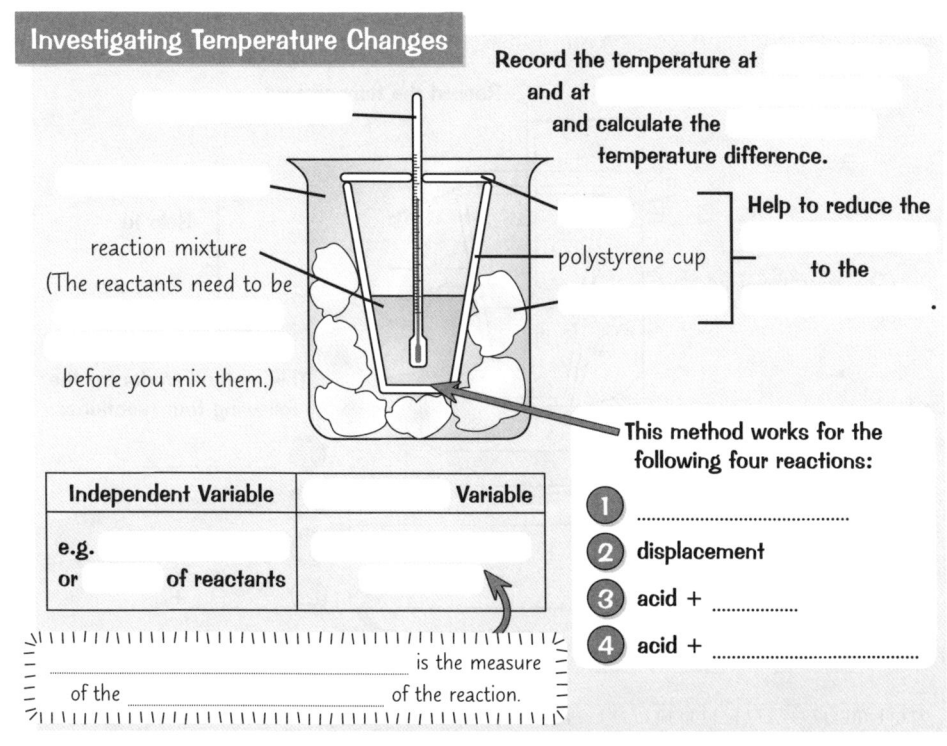

Investigating Temperature Changes

Record the temperature at .... and at .... and calculate the temperature difference.

reaction mixture
(The reactants need to be .... before you mix them.)

polystyrene cup

Help to reduce the .... to the ....

This method works for the following four reactions:
1. ....
2. .... displacement
3. acid + ...
4. acid + ...

Independent Variable	.... Variable
e.g. .... or .... of reactants	

.... is the measure of the .... of the reaction.

Required Practicals 2

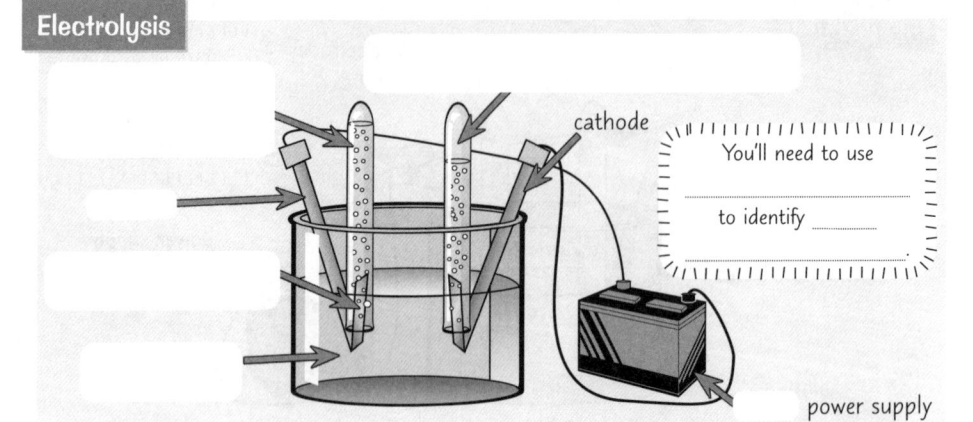

Second Go: ...../...../.....

Electrolysis

cathode

You'll need to use .... to identify ....

power supply

Product at	Product at
Either	Either

Investigating Temperature Changes

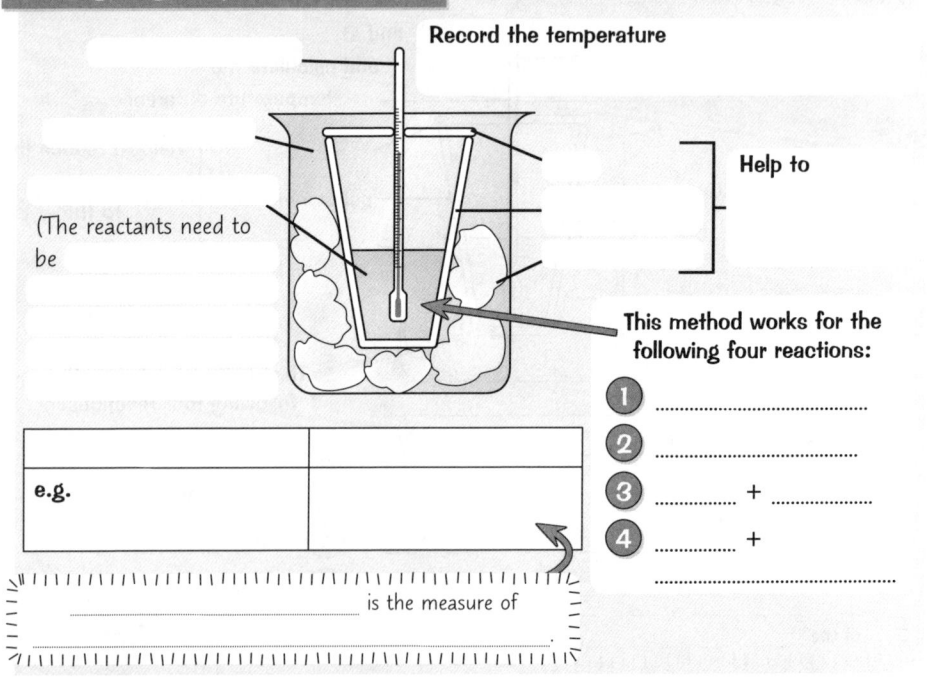

Record the temperature

Help to

(The reactants need to be

e.g.	

.... is the measure of ....

This method works for the following four reactions:

1. ....
2. ....
3. .... + ...
4. .... + ...

Required Practicals

Required Practicals 3

First Go: ..... / ..... / .....

Two Ways of Measuring Rates of Reaction

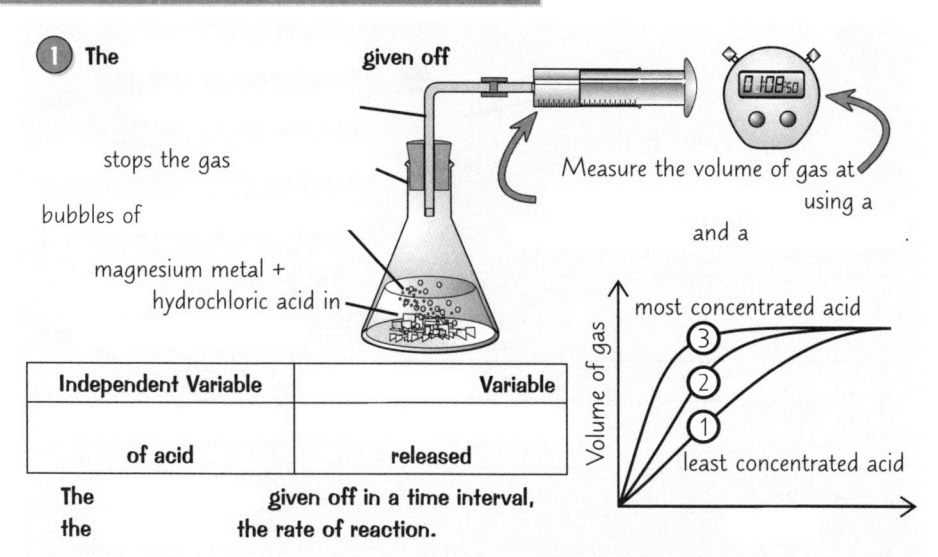

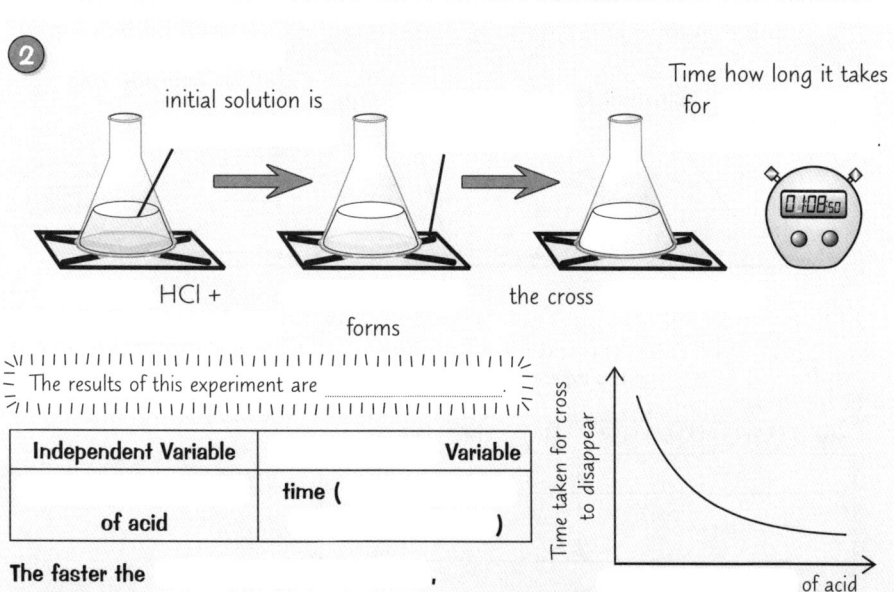

1 The _____ given off _____

stops the gas bubbles of _____

magnesium metal + hydrochloric acid in _____

Measure the volume of gas at _____ using a _____ and a _____.

Independent Variable	_____ Variable
_____ of acid	_____ released

The _____ given off in a time interval, the _____ the rate of reaction.

most concentrated acid
least concentrated acid
Volume of gas

2

initial solution is _____

HCl + _____

the cross _____ forms

Time how long it takes for _____

The results of this experiment are _____.

Independent Variable	_____ Variable
_____ of acid	time (_____)

The faster the _____, the faster the _____.

The experiments show that a _____ gives a _____.

Time taken for cross to disappear
_____ of acid

Required Practicals

144

Second Go: ...../...../.....

Required Practicals 3

Two Ways of Measuring Rates of Reaction

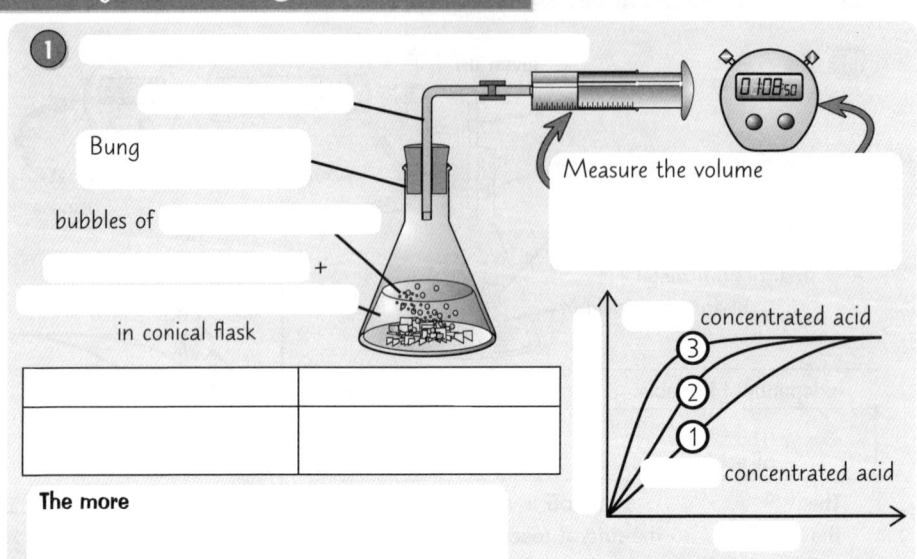

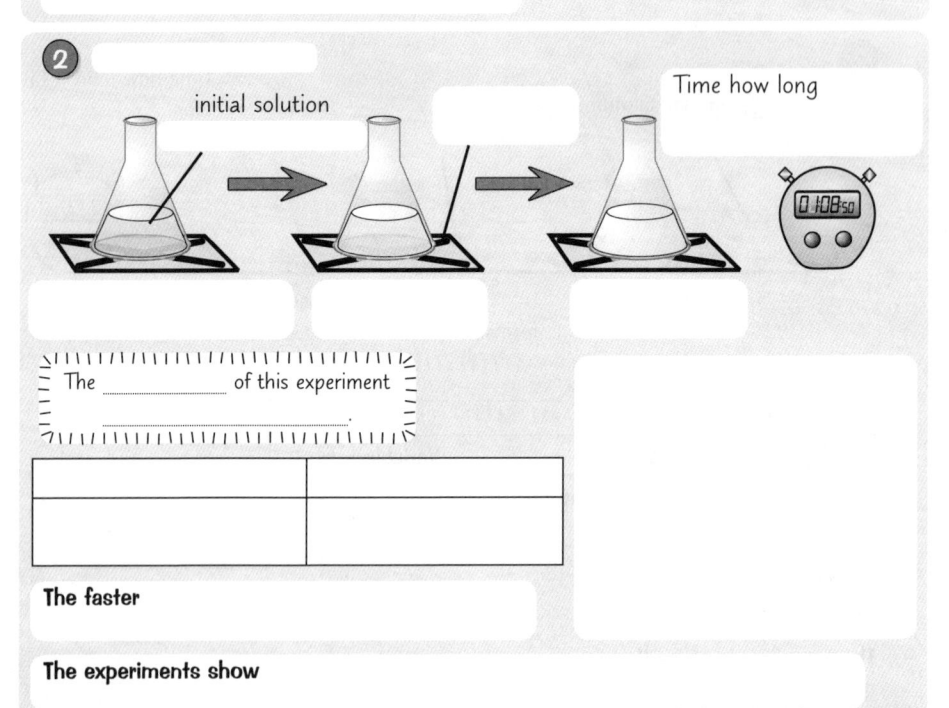

①

Bung

bubbles of

_____ + _____

in conical flask

Measure the volume

The more

concentrated acid

③
②
①

concentrated acid

②

initial solution

Time how long

The _____ of this experiment _____ .

The faster

The experiments show

Required Practicals

Required Practicals 4

First Go: ..... / ..... / .....

Paper Chromatography

R_f values are _____. To compare them, you have to use _____.

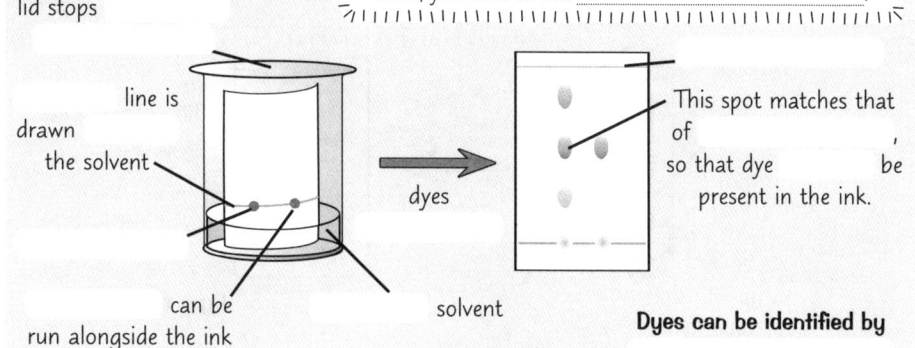

lid stops _____

_____ line is drawn _____ the solvent _____

_____ dyes

_____ can be run alongside the ink

_____ solvent

This spot matches that of _____, so that dye _____ be present in the ink.

Dyes can be identified by _____ to known compounds.

The experiment should _____ to see if the spots still match in _____.

Identifying Ions

dropping pipette

Add a _____ of reagent.

_____ mystery

Anion	Test	Observation
Cl⁻	Add dilute _____, then silver nitrate solution	_____ precipitate
		_____ precipitate
		yellow precipitate
SO_4^{2-}	Add _____, then _____ solution	
CO_3^{2-}	Add _____ the test tube to a test tube of limewater.	limewater _____

Some metal ions form a _____ with NaOH solution.

Ca^{2+}	white
Cu^{2+}	
	green
Fe^{3+}	
	white

Precipitate _____ in excess NaOH to form a _____

Four steps for performing flame tests

1. Dip a _____ loop in _____.
2. Hold it in a _____ Bunsen flame until it burns _____.
3. Dip the loop into the sample.
4. Hold the loop in _____.

Li⁺	Na⁺		
crimson		lilac	orange-red

Required Practicals

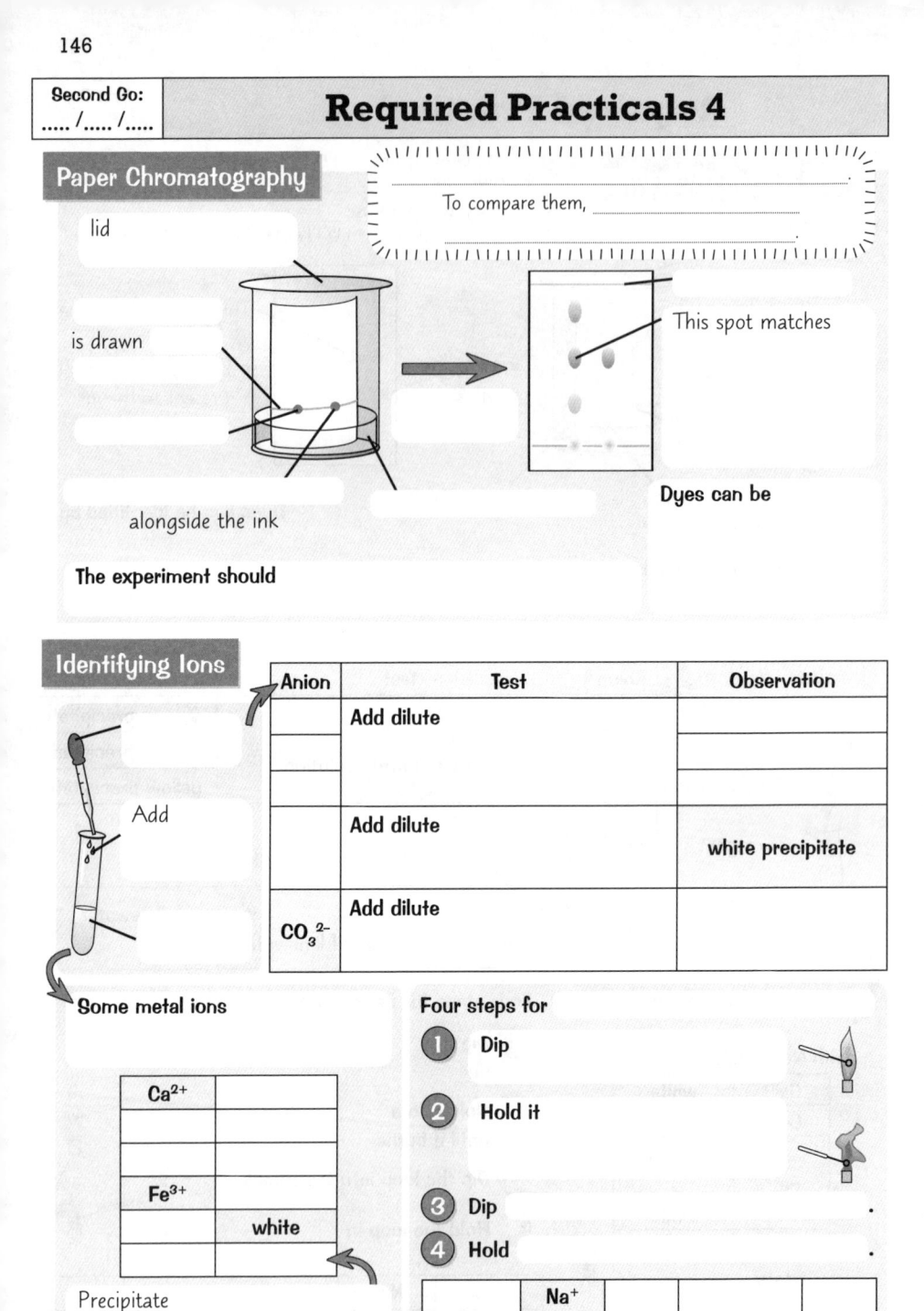

Second Go: ..../..../....

Required Practicals 4

Paper Chromatography

lid

To compare them, ...

is drawn

This spot matches

alongside the ink

Dyes can be

The experiment should

Identifying Ions

Anion	Test	Observation
	Add dilute	
	Add dilute	white precipitate
CO_3^{2-}	Add dilute	

Add

Some metal ions

Ca^{2+}	
Fe^{3+}	
	white

Precipitate

Four steps for
1. Dip
2. Hold it
3. Dip
4. Hold

	Na^+		
crimson		lilac	

Required Practicals

Required Practicals 5

First Go: ...../...../.....

Five Steps for the Purification of Water

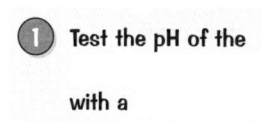

1 Test the pH of the _____ with a _____

2 _____ the sample (if needed) via _____. Use a _____ indicator will _____ in the _____ — _____ the sample.

3 Test for the presence of _____.

Do a flame test for _____ ions. _____ flame

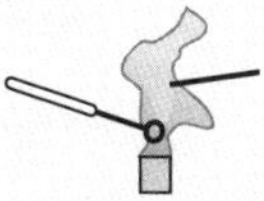

Use dilute _____ test for _____ precipitate

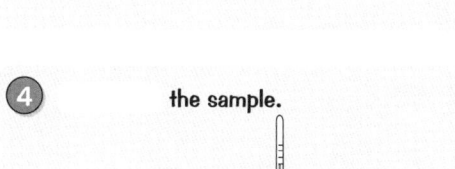

_____ and _____ solution to _____ ions.

4 _____ the sample.

_____ and _____ to the condenser.

Water

Condenser — the vapour turns back _____ here as it is _____.

Water

Any dissolved _____ will be _____.

_____ water

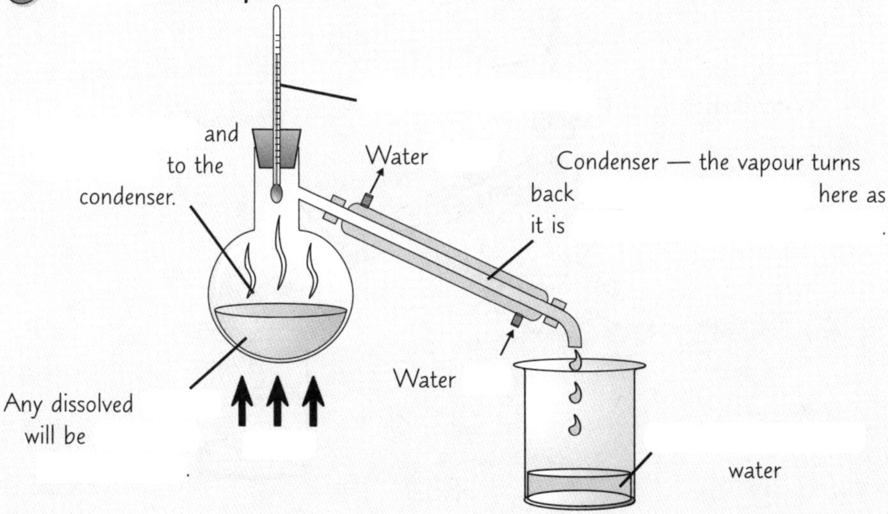

5 _____ the pH of the _____ water, and for the presence of _____.

Required Practicals

Required Practicals 5

Second Go: ...../...../.....

Five Steps for the Purification of Water

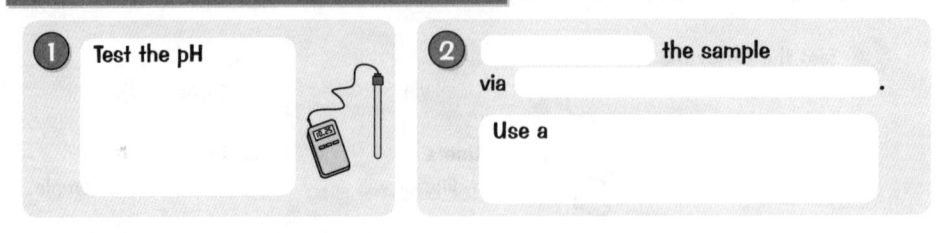

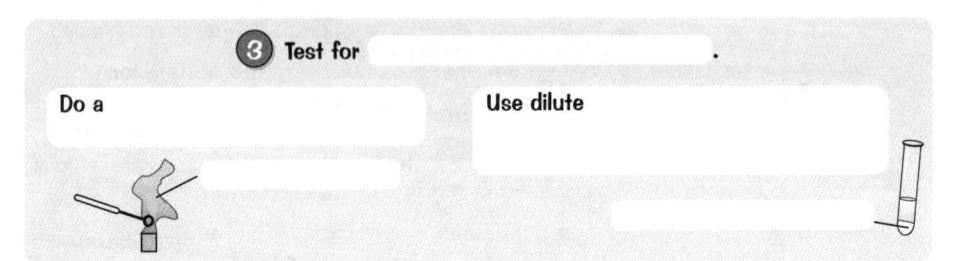

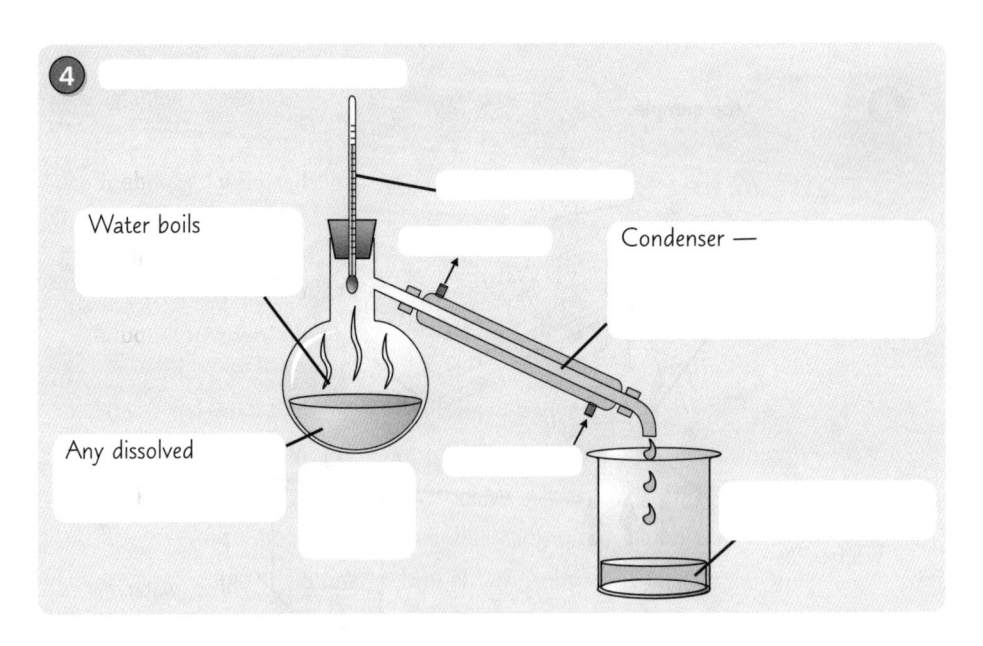

1 Test the pH

2 _____ the sample via _____.
Use a _____

3 Test for _____.

Do a _____

Use dilute _____

4 _____

Water boils

Condenser —

Any dissolved

5 Retest the pH

Required Practicals

Mixed Practice Quizzes

Feeling practical after p.139-148? Don't worry — you won't have to build any flat-pack furniture or anything like that. Just see how you get on with these quizzes.

Quiz 1 Date: ...... / ...... / ......

1) How can you measure the volume of gas produced in a reaction?
2) When should you stop adding the solution from the burette during a titration?
3) What type of power supply is used for electrolysis?
4) Where should the pencil line in chromatography be relative to the solvent?
5) Why is cotton wool often used in experiments measuring temperature change?
6) Describe a test used to confirm whether a sample contains sulfate ions.
7) How does distillation separate water from dissolved salts?
8) True or false? When making a soluble salt from an insoluble metal compound, the excess solid is removed by evaporation.
9) Why might chemical tests be used in an electrolysis experiment?
10) Describe what to do before dipping a loop into a sample for a flame test.

Total:

Quiz 2 Date: ...... / ...... / ......

1) True or false? The concentration of reactants could be the independent variable when investigating the temperature change of a reaction.
2) Give one limitation of the method for measuring the rate of precipitation formation where a cross is observed through a reaction vessel.
3) What should be considered when choosing an insoluble metal compound for making a particular soluble salt?
4) How do you test for the presence of carbonate ions in a sample?
5) How could you dry the solid product of crystallisation?
6) How close should titration results be in order to be considered consistent?
7) Give one test you could use on distilled water to assess its purity.
8) What name is given to a solution that is undergoing electrolysis?
9) Give two possible dependent variables for measuring the rate of a reaction.
10) True or false? Halides all behave the same in acidified silver nitrate solution.

Total:

Required Practicals

Mixed Practice Quizzes

Quiz 3 Date: ...... / ...... / ......

1) Describe how to fill the burette with acid when preparing a titration.
2) What can you say about the rate of a reaction compared to another if it produces more gas in the same time period?
3) Describe how to collect the gaseous products of electrolysis.
4) How could you confirm the presence of a certain dye in a mixture if it matches the spot from a pure dye in a chromatogram?
5) Give two types of insoluble metal compound used to make soluble salts.
6) Describe how to measure the temperature change of a reaction mixture.
7) What could you use to measure the pH of water during water purification?
8) Suggest three ways to minimise energy loss from a reaction mixture.
9) What is observed when NaOH solution is added to a solution of Cu^{2+} ions?
10) What is the role of the condenser during the distillation of water?

Total:

Quiz 4 Date: ...... / ...... / ......

1) Give two types of reaction suitable for a temperature change investigation.
2) True or false? When carrying out a titration, the solution with an unknown concentration should be in the burette.
3) When making soluble salts, which step follows the filtration step?
4) How does increasing the concentration of hydrochloric acid (HCl) affect the rate of its reaction with sodium thiosulfate?
5) Why might a lid be used in a chromatography experiment?
6) Give two examples of products that can form at the cathode in electrolysis.
7) How can you test for the presence of NaCl in a water sample?
8) Describe how to measure a volume of a solution added from a burette.
9) How can you tell apart a precipitate of $Al(OH)_3$ from other white metal hydroxide precipitates?
10) True or false? R_f values can only be compared if the same solvent has been used.

Total:

Required Practicals

Practical Skills

Apparatus and Techniques

First Go:
..... / ..... / .....

Measuring Mass

substance to be

container (set to   )

Transferring solid to   :
When making a solution, remaining solid
out of the   with
the   .

or

Find the   of the
container and   before and
after you   .

Three Ways to Measure Liquids

① Pipette   transfers

(draws up liquid)   volumes
                        calibrated to
                        reduce transfer
pipette   errors

③ Measuring

Pick a

for volume required.

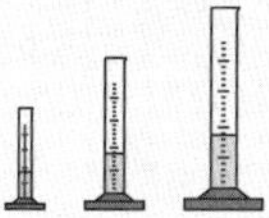

When measuring   :
Always read the volume from the
of the   .

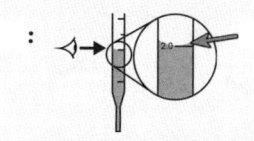

② Burette

                                scale measures
Volume of liquid   from
used is the

                        the
                        initial and final
                        on
                        the scale.

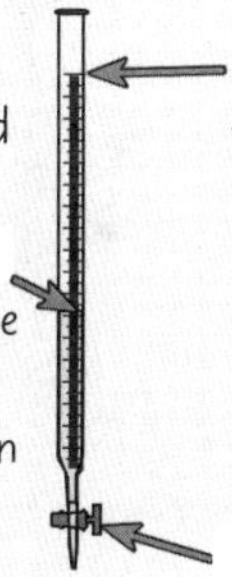

                                        into
                                        a container

Measuring Time

              are

              the timer
at   right time

Measuring Temperature

                    wait for
                    temperature to

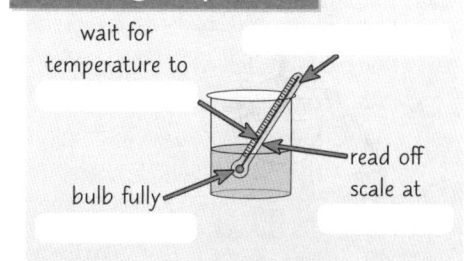

                                    read off
                                    scale at
bulb fully

Practical Skills

Apparatus and Techniques

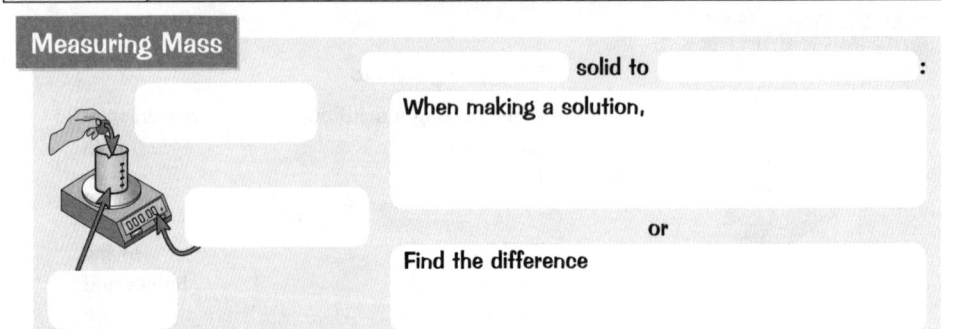

Second Go: ..... / ..... / .....

Measuring Mass

_____ solid to _____ :

When making a solution, _____

or

Find the difference _____

Three Ways to Measure Liquids

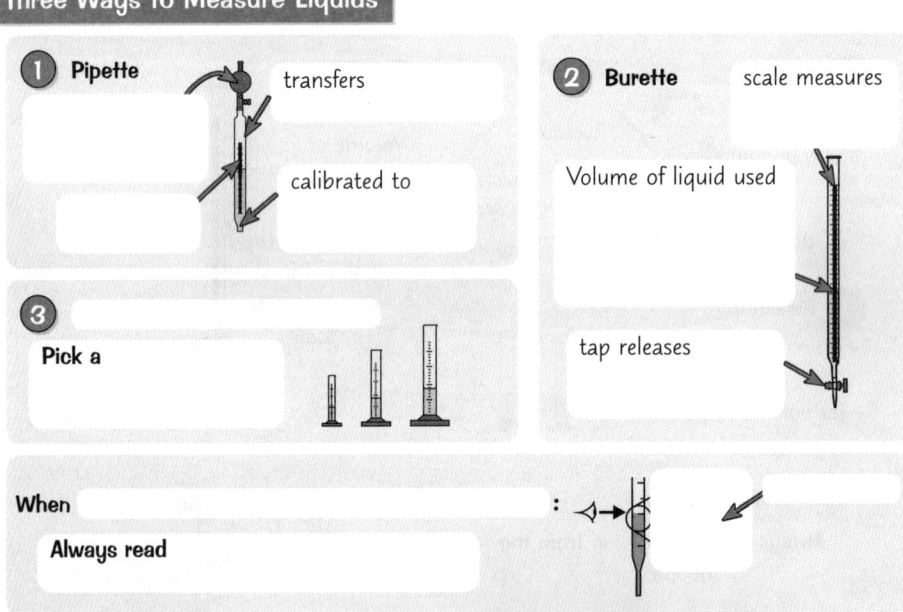

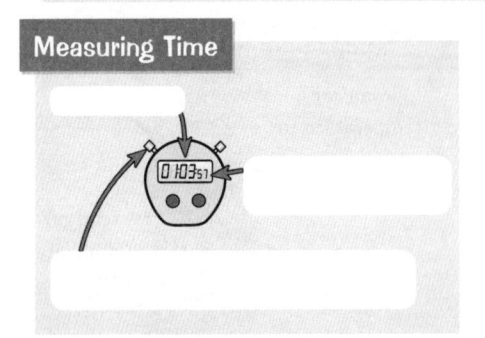

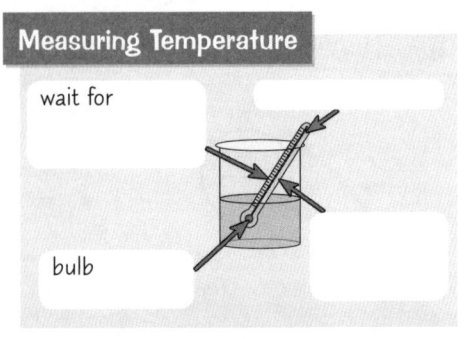

1 Pipette

transfers _____

calibrated to _____

2 Burette

scale measures _____

Volume of liquid used _____

tap releases _____

3 _____

Pick a _____

When _____ :

Always read _____

Measuring Time

Measuring Temperature

wait for _____

bulb _____

Practical Skills

Practical Techniques

First Go:
...../...../.....

Measuring pH

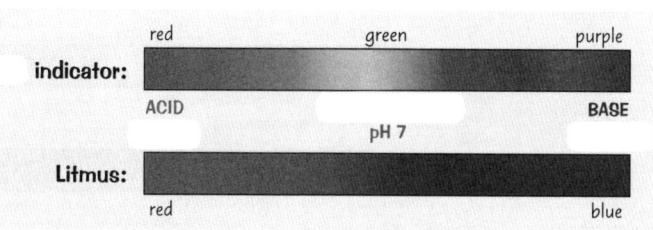

_____ indicator:
red — green — purple
ACID — pH 7 — BASE

Litmus:
red — blue

Indicator solution	Indicator _____
Changes colour of _____	For testing _____ of solution
Good for showing the _____ in titrations	Use _____ to test gases

pH probes and _____ give a _____ value for pH.

Safety Precautions

_____ to do with your method _____ you start any experiment.

Use a _____ when _____

Use a fume cupboard to avoid _____ like chlorine.

Wear a lab coat, _____ to avoid spillages.

_____ and _____ to protect against _____ or _____ chemicals.

Work in a _____ area.

Use a _____ to transfer solids.

Don't handle _____ directly.

When _____ a liquid, add the _____ to the _____.

Keep _____ away from _____.

Practical Skills

Second Go:
..... / ..... / .....

Practical Techniques

Measuring pH

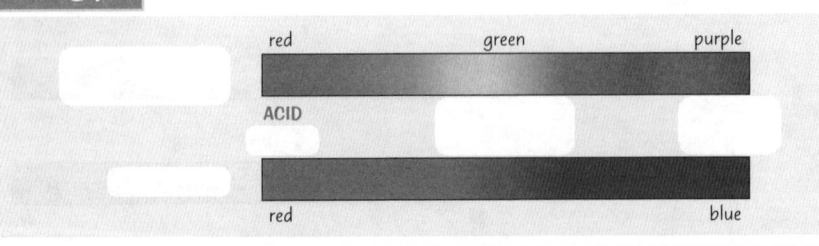

red   green   purple

ACID

red   blue

Indicator solution	
Changes	For testing
Good for	Use

pH probes and

Safety Precautions

Read the

Wear a

Use a

_____ to avoid releasing _____

Don't handle

Work in a

Use a

When diluting

away from

Practical Skills

Equipment and Heating Substances

First Go: ..... / ..... / .....

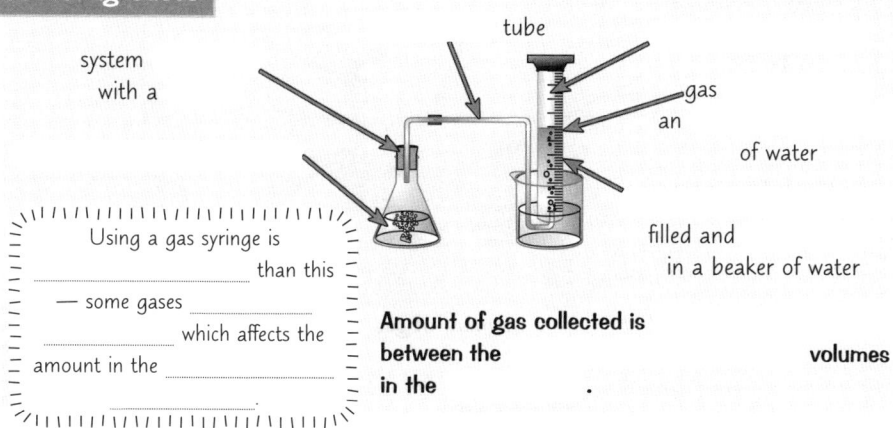

Collecting Gases

system with a ...... tube

...... gas
an ...... of water

Using a gas syringe is ...... than this — some gases ...... which affects the amount in the ......

...... filled and ...... in a beaker of water

Amount of gas collected is ...... between the ...... in the ...... volumes ......

Using Bunsen Burners

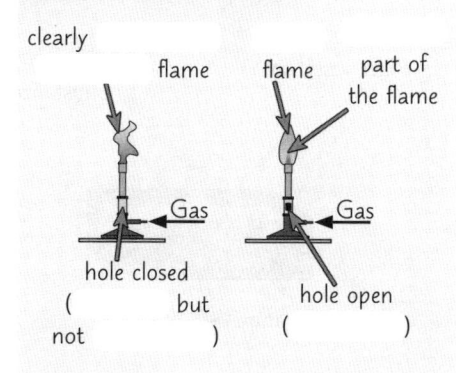

clearly ......
...... flame   ...... flame   ...... part of the flame

← Gas   ← Gas

hole closed (...... but not ......)

hole open (......)

You can use ...... to show how apparatus is ...... :

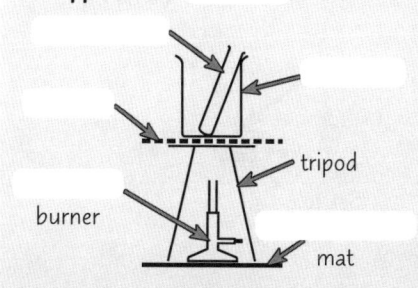

...... burner
...... tripod
...... mat

Other Heating Methods

Water bath

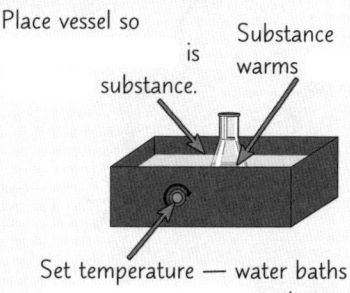

Place vessel so ...... is ...... substance.

Substance warms ......

Set temperature — water baths ...... to heat ......

Electric heater

Vessel heats ......

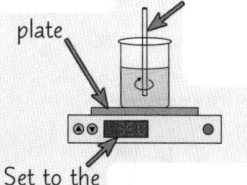

...... plate

Set to the ...... temperature — it can go ......

Equipment and Heating Substances

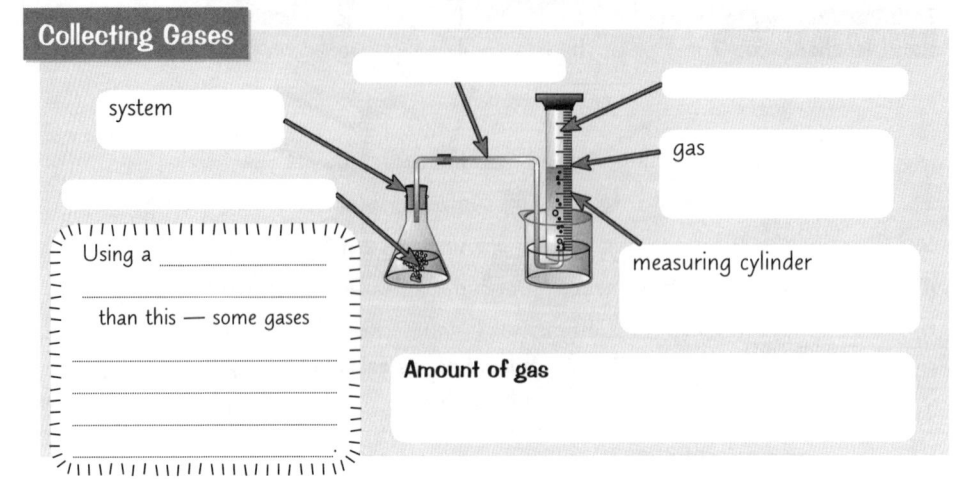

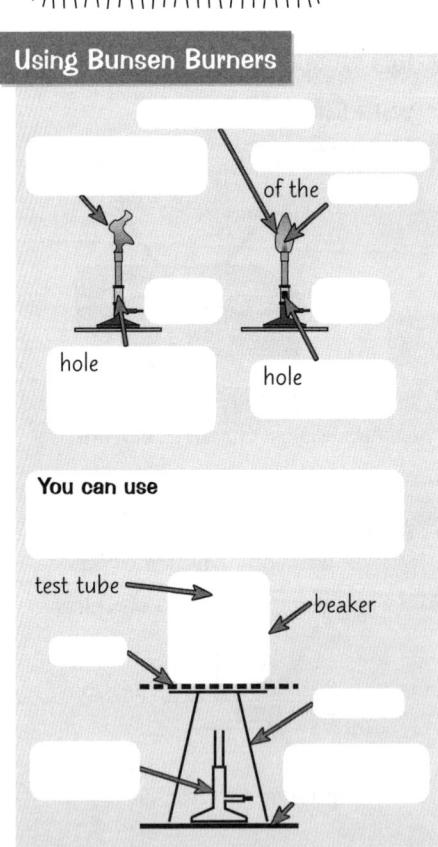

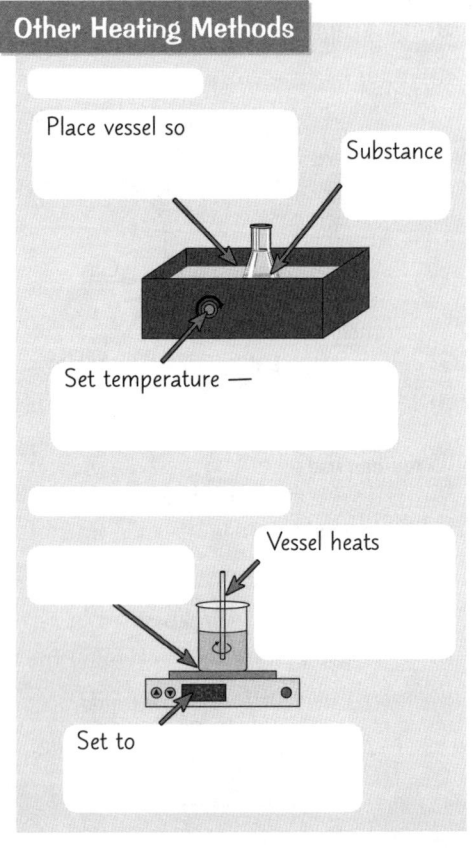

Second Go: ..... / ..... / .....

Collecting Gases

system

Using a .... than this — some gases ....

gas

measuring cylinder

Amount of gas

Using Bunsen Burners

.... of the ....

hole

hole

You can use

test tube

beaker

Other Heating Methods

Place vessel so ....

Substance ....

Set temperature —

Vessel heats ....

Set to ....

Practical Skills

Mixed Practice Quizzes

The final quiz pages of the book... Hooray! Before you start celebrating, use them to check you know all of the practical skills covered on p.151-156.

Quiz 1 — Date: ...... / ...... / ......

1) Give two examples of when you'd use indicator paper.
2) How is liquid released from a burette into a container?
3) Give one way you can ensure you are working safely with hot glassware.
4) Describe how to use a measuring cylinder to collect gaseous products.
5) Outline how to measure the mass of a substance using a mass balance.
6) Give one piece of equipment you could use to transfer solid chemicals safely.
7) How can you ensure that a sample is heated evenly by an electric heater?
8) Give an example of when a scientific drawing may be used.
9) True or false? You should measure the temperature of a solution immediately after placing a thermometer in it.
10) Why might using a gas syringe to measure the volume of gas be more accurate than an upturned measuring cylinder?

Total:

Quiz 2 — Date: ...... / ...... / ......

1) Describe how to read the volume of a liquid from a scale.
2) What piece of apparatus could you use to measure temperature?
3) Give an advantage of using a pH probe and meter over universal indicator.
4) What is the hottest part of a Bunsen burner flame?
5) Give two ways of heating a sample without using a flame.
6) Give an advantage of using a pipette to transfer a specific volume of liquid.
7) Give a safety precaution you should follow when using flammable chemicals.
8) What is the neutral pH value?
9) Give two methods of collecting the volume of gas produced in a reaction.
10) Give three protective items that should be worn when carrying out an experiment.

Total:

Practical Skills

Mixed Practice Quizzes

Quiz 3   Date: ...... / ...... / ......

1) Give an example of when you might use an indicator solution.
2) Describe how a Bunsen burner should look when it is alight but not heating.
3) Give two ways of accurately transferring a mass of solid to a reaction vessel.
4) How do you work out the volume of liquid added from a burette?
5) True or false? Water baths and electric heaters both warm substances evenly.
6) How can you avoid releasing harmful gases in a reaction into the room?
7) Describe how to accurately measure the temperature of a solution.
8) What piece of apparatus can transfer a specific volume of liquid?
9) What can be used help to seal a system when collecting the gaseous products of a reaction in a filled, upturned measuring cylinder?
10) Compare the heating capabilities of water baths and electric heaters.

Total:

Quiz 4   Date: ...... / ...... / ......

1) What piece of equipment could you use to measure time?
2) True of false? Damp indicator paper can be used to test gases.
3) How could you make sure that all of a solid substance from a weighing container is transferred to a reaction vessel?
4) True or false? When diluting a liquid, add the water to the concentrated substance.
5) How should you place a vessel in a water bath so that its contents are heated evenly?
6) What must be considered when picking a suitably sized measuring cylinder?
7) How should the hole on a Bunsen burner be set when it is used for heating?
8) Give three ways to measure the pH of a solution.
9) How does bubbling gas into a measuring cylinder that has been filled and upturned in a beaker of water allow you to measure its volume?
10) Give one example of when and why you might use a funnel in an experiment.

Total: